D0395042

THE
ETERNAL
PARTY

The eternal party :
understanding my dad,
Larry Hagman, the TV
star America loved to
hate
33305236554915
6an   07/07/16

THE
ETERNAL
PARTY

*Understanding My Dad, Larry Hagman,
the TV Star America Loved to Hate*

Kristina Hagman
with Elizabeth Kaye

Thomas Dunne Books ♏ St. Martin's Press New York

THOMAS DUNNE BOOKS.
An imprint of St. Martin's Press.

THE ETERNAL PARTY. Copyright © 2016 by Kristina Hagman. All rights reserved.
Printed in the United States of America. For information, address St. Martin's Press,
175 Fifth Avenue, New York, N.Y. 10010.

www.thomasdunnebooks.com
www.stmartins.com

Designed by Steven Seighman

Library of Congress Cataloging-in-Publication Data

Names: Hagman, Kristina, author. | Kaye, Elizabeth, 1945– author.
Title: The eternal party : understanding my dad, Larry Hagman, the TV star
  America loved to hate / Kristina Hagman with Elizabeth Kaye.
Description: First edition. | New York : Thomas Dunne Books, 2016.
Identifiers: LCCN 2015051258| ISBN 9781250076762 (hardback) |
  ISBN 9781466888340 (e-book)
Subjects: LCSH: Hagman, Larry. | Actors—United States—Biography. | Hagman,
  Kristina. | Fathers and daughters—United States—Biography. | BISAC:
  BIOGRAPHY & AUTOBIOGRAPHY / Entertainment & Performing Arts. |
  BIOGRAPHY & AUTOBIOGRAPHY / Personal Memoirs.
Classification: LCC PN2287.H17 H34 2016 | DDC 791.4502/8092—dc23
LC record available at http://lccn.loc.gov/2015051258

Our books may be purchased in bulk for promotional, educational, or business use.
Please contact your local bookseller or the Macmillan Corporate and Premium
Sales Department at 1-800-221-7945, extension 5442, or by e-mail at Macmillan
SpecialMarkets@macmillan.com.

First Edition: June 2016

10   9   8   7   6   5   4   3   2   1

For
my mom and dad
and
my wonderful supportive children, Kaya and Nora,
whose own amazing stories are unfolding

Author's Note

This is a true story, though some names and details have been changed.

Contents

Writing a book . . . compels you to want to sum up your life . . . I'm not going to give in to that urge. Let someone else sum up my life when it's over.

—*LARRY HAGMAN, IN THE POSTSCRIPT TO HIS AUTOBIOGRAPHY*

THE

ETERNAL

PARTY

1
—

Dad's Last Day

I T WAS THE MORNING after Thanksgiving, and everything had changed. Dad was still in the Dallas hospital room where my brother, Preston, and I had sat beside him for the last two days. But now there was no doubt that he was dying. My father had been close to death several times before. On one of those occasions, I was so sure we were losing him that I had cried nonstop until my mother told me, "That's enough. He'll get better." I thought she was delusional. But within a week he was well again, and I understood that I still had things to learn from my mother: she never gave up on Dad, nor should I. But this time was different. This time he was not going to recover.

He had been still and quiet in the middle of the night when I left him in Preston's care while I went back to the hotel to get some sleep. As I had promised my brother I would, I returned as the sun was coming up over the Dallas skyline. Amazingly, I had been able to sleep for a few hours. I felt ready to face and to cope with what was about to happen.

When I entered my father's room in the intensive care unit, I could see him turning and tossing. I immediately sensed his agitation and fear. He was talking a mile a minute, words pouring out of him, fast, as if he had so many things he needed to say while he was still able to say them.

He had been like this for some time, Preston said. We exchanged a few words before he left, utterly exhausted, hoping to get a bit of rest.

I approached the bed and stroked my father's forehead. I moistened his cracked lips and leaned into him, straining to understand what he was saying. His words came out jumbled. He seemed to go from mood to mood, changing inflections and even accents, and tossing in a giggle now and then. Though much of what he said was unintelligible, I could easily make out the two words he repeated breathlessly, over and over again. The words were: forgive me.

Why was he saying this? Did he mean those words for me? For my brother, who had just left? Was he asking forgiveness from some higher power? Whatever he meant, the words made me deeply sad. Anyone who has sat by the deathbed of a loved one knows the profound sense of sorrow you feel when you know there is nothing you can do that will make them better. You want to share every precious moment with them; you long to comfort them in any way possible.

As I sat on the bed and held him in that hospital room, I was taken back to a time when he had comforted me. I was eight years old when I was knocked unconscious because a horse had kicked me and sent me flying into a fence on which I'd hit my head. I was unconscious for three days but vividly recall coming to for just an instant when Dad was cradling me in his arms as he ran down the hospital corridor. I know he stayed with me day and night until I was well enough to come home. He would never leave me by myself in a cold, institutional hospital. So now I tried to reassure him, to reach him, so he would know he was not alone.

But I had a surreal thought: though I could touch his failing body, I was not sure he was in that hospital room at all. His consciousness was somewhere else. He called out to my mother, "Maj, we have to do this . . . Majsy, let's go . . ." I wished my mother could have been with him. She loved him so much, but by then, she was far too debilitated by Alzheimer's disease to even be told of his condition.

Every few minutes the nurse would come in to measure his oxygen level. "Take a deep breath for me, Larry," she would say in her sweet Texas accent, but he just kept talking, talking, talking. He addressed his own mother, who had been dead for twenty-two years. "I will, Mom. Sure, Mom . . ." and then more words I could not decipher.

From that point on, the only words I could make out were the words he just kept saying over and over, "Forgive me . . . forgive me . . . forgive me."

I had sat alone with my father in intensive care twice since his liver transplant nearly twenty years ago. On those other occasions when he seemed close to death, I had made sure to tell him I loved him, to let him know that I had seen him struggle in his marriage and I too knew how hard that could be; I told him about my hopes and fears for my children and my desire to get back to being an artist when they were old enough to stand on their own. Most of all, I let him know how grateful I was to him for holding me so close my entire life. On those occasions, I had said everything I wanted and needed to say, and now there was nothing more I longed to tell him, nothing had been left unsaid. We had done the hard work of sounding each other's emotions. Now the only words I wanted to say were words that would put him at peace. I told him everybody loved him, and the image of Dad surrounded by his lovely granddaughters came to mind; I told him they adored him. Three of them were Preston's daughters, two were mine, and we had brought them to his hospital room just yesterday, before his condition turned dire. When they had arrived in Dallas a few days ago, they had been so excited to see him, crowding into the room and sitting on the bed with Granpa to tell him all their news. When we visited him again, we knew for sure that Granpa Larry was not going to join us for the Thanksgiving dinner he had so carefully planned. That day, each of his granddaughters had the chance to be alone with him.

Dad was delighted by these five lovely girls; he called them the Blondies. He loved being with them. He had not been the kind of grandfather who came to school sporting events or did projects with them. He just liked having them around at breakfast or cuddling with them on the couch to watch TV. He saw them as his team of beautiful girls. But I knew each of them well enough to understand that they would want to be recognized as individuals; it was important that each of them got to experience some time alone with him. Anyone who knew Dad well knew how wonderful it felt to have his whole attention. He had the ability to make you feel like the most important person in the world. Whatever he said would be theirs alone to know and reflect on in the coming years. For me, these private visits were lovely and bittersweet because I sensed this would be the last time he would be able to talk to them.

While each girl had her visit with Granpa, the rest of us sat on the floor outside his room. The nurses and the hospital staff were great, accommodating us by walking over our outstretched legs that took up the entire hallway. We were like some ancient tribe camped out in the hospital corridor, awaiting the next opportunity to visit with our king.

But now, there was only him and me and the words he repeated over and over: "Forgive me . . . forgive me."

What was going on in his mind? Where was he? I seldom feel helpless, but I felt totally helpless as I held him, knowing there was nothing more his doctors could do for him and all too aware that it was left to me to ease his mind. As a mother, I had always been able to find a way to comfort my children. Now I prayed those instincts would guide me to find the way to comfort my father. But no matter what I did, his agitation and monologue continued. I straightened his sheets, cooled and kissed his feverish forehead, put a wet towel to his lips. Again, I was taken back to memories from the distant past: I found myself thinking of how he had slept beside my bed to care for me when I had been sick with the chicken pox at three years old. He had been so worried that I would scratch my face in my sleep and leave permanent scars that he had made me wear gloves day and night. If I unconsciously pulled the gloves off, he gently distracted me and put them back on again. This was my dad, the man who often demanded my absolute attention and obedience but who could also be completely and self-lessly giving. Whatever Dad's flaws, he understood what love is.

I had to do something for him! When my children were distressed, I had often sung them to sleep, and so I sang the same soothing songs to Dad: "Swing Low, Sweet Chariot" and "Amazing Grace." After that, I could see by observing his breathing that he had relaxed a bit, and I was encouraged to sing more.

It came to me that Dad and I had been singing together only a month earlier at the New York memorial for our dear friend, the artist Barton Benes. The words to that song were fresh in my mind: "I'll be loving you always, with a love that's true always . . ."

As I continued singing, something amazing happened. It was as if his delirium had lifted. Without opening his eyes, Dad joined his weak and trembling voice with mine, "Days may not be fair always . . . that's when I'll be there always . . . not for just a minute, not for just an hour, not for just a year but . . . alllllllwayyyyys."

It was such an uplifting moment that despite my knowledge that he was in total organ failure, I caught myself thinking he might come back to us, that he would magically sit up and say, "Just kidding!" I could not help but wish he was pulling another one of the practical jokes he was famous for. But then he began asking for forgiveness again. Searching for another way to soothe him, I said, "I forgive you." But my words did not penetrate.

Throughout my life, Dad's indomitable spirit brought all of us so much happiness. He had often been able to turn a depressing situation into a joke that would make us all laugh at ourselves for being down or serious. Being glum was never a part of Dad's game plan. For example, when he had visited his own mother in the hospital before she died, instead of searching for the right thing to say to her, they had whistled a Bach cantata together.

Because he had such a mischievous way about him, people would laugh at his antics instead of taking offense. If a woman came up to the table and asked to have her photo taken with him, he would play-fully grab her breast just as the camera flash went off, leaving her with a picture that was not like any other celebrity photo. He was like a wayward but charming child who was never going to separate right from wrong. Dad was like Peter Pan in a man's body; he had never wanted to grow up. What good were grown-up, serious words to him? So I smiled at him, and I was so filled with loving feelings for him that I found myself speaking to him as if he were my son.

I said, "You're a very good boy."

The words even surprised me. I didn't know where they came from, but those must have been the words he needed to hear because, after that, he never spoke again. The constant asking for forgiveness had ended.

Though he was quiet, I could see from the way he grimaced and the way his body was contorted that he was in severe pain. When the nurse returned, she said I should ask the doctor to give him morphine. I told her I did not feel comfortable making that request.

"You have experience with what is done at the end of life," I said. "If you think Dad needs morphine, could you ask the doctor for it?"

Within minutes, the doctor arrived. He examined Dad briefly, then ordered the morphine, which was administered right away, and I soon watched the tension in Dad's body begin to ease. As his breath became more profound, I found myself taking fuller, deeper breaths along with him. But as the relaxation transformed his body, I realized that this change also meant that what little bit of his consciousness had remained was now gone forever.

Dad had been silent for a while when his girlfriend, who was just my age, came into the room. She looked like the millionaire she was: her dark hair coiffed, her makeup and nails perfect. She was dressed in skintight jeans, a flatteringly elegant shirt, and high-heeled boots. She was not at all like my mother, who was a few years older than Dad and had gained some weight over the last few years and wore minimal makeup and had towel-dried, frosty-white hair.

As the girlfriend crawled into bed with Dad, I could not help but note the irony of her timing. She came as soon as the tumult and the work of caring for him was over.

"Lukey honey," she said in her purring Southern drawl, "squeeze mah hand if you know Ah'm here."

He did not respond; she became more insistent. She was a woman who got what she wanted, and she was determined to get a response from him. I understood her desire. Hadn't I been doing the same thing for hours? But now, with his urgent pleas silenced, I could feel how much that effort had taken out of me, and I was spent and grateful that he was calm at last.

I watched them together for a while. Dad couldn't squeeze her hand or do anything else. He had gone from talking a mile a minute to barely breathing. Trying another way to reach him she placed her iPhone beside his ear and turned the volume up on what she said was his favorite music. "Sound is the last thing to go, you know," she said with authority.

"Yes," I answered quietly. "But I don't think he can hear it."

I was not familiar with the music she played; it must have been their favorite music together. It struck me that Dad had so many different lives, and I knew very little about this one. Dad had kept her a secret from me for about two years. The secrecy had made a wedge between us, separating us until he discovered I did not condemn him for his relationship with her, and we began doing things together again. I had been so relieved to be back in Dad's life, and I was grateful that his girlfriend had not shut me out. I felt it was time to return the favor and let her be alone with him. I left the room. Maybe the presence of a loved one was the last thing to go, and Dad had recently told me that he loved her.

While they were alone in the room, Preston came back to the hospital bringing all our daughters with him. We were all close by as Dad slipped further away. Then Dad's *Dallas* costars Patrick Duffy and Linda Gray joined us to give their support. They had long been two of his dearest friends. They had been watching out for him since the new

Dallas had started shooting a year earlier. Linda had given him dietary advice. Patrick was always the guy who teamed up with Dad to play pranks on the set and in recent weeks had begun to stand by him at public functions as Dad became frailer, always ready to offer a steady hand in case he needed it. Patrick helped Dad in such a gracious way, a way that Dad could accept it since it was never obvious or embarrassing.

Having been through the last few hours with Dad, I knew he would not open his eyes ever again. I felt raw; I needed the solace of privacy. It was just after 3:00 P.M. when I kissed my father for the last time. He was peaceful and seemingly unaware as the final scene of his life played out, the actor surrounded by an audience of those who loved him.

The granddaughters must have sensed it was time for quiet too, and they all came back to the hotel with me. After hugging them repeatedly, I went to my own room and sat alone. I was trying to absorb what I had just gone through and face the fact that I would never be with my father again.

Preston stayed with Dad until he took his final breath. He said that breath came at 4:20 P.M. This particular time was significant because 420 is the unofficial symbol for the use and appreciation of one of Dad's favorite substances: marijuana.

When Preston told me this I thought, *Just as Dad would want it— scripted to the end.*

2

A Forensic Study: The Search for My Father

RECENTLY, I WAS SENT a photograph of my dad that made me smile and tear up at the same time. He is walking on the beach, wearing a loose white shirt and white pants. His arms are wide open, his palms turned up, and he looks so happy; it's a peaceful happiness, a contented happiness, the happiness of a man who had known what he wanted and got it.

Because I had been very close to my dad, when I was with him that contentment washed over me. We always stayed in touch, sometimes unintentionally; for example, he butt-dialed me all the time. I would get a call out of the blue as I was shopping at the grocery store. I would say, "Hello . . . Hi, Dad . . . Are you there?"

I would get no reply, and then as I was standing in front of cans of soup in California, I would hear the sound of a party at full tilt, going on somewhere in Texas.

Earlier when I lived in Seattle with my husband and daughters, Dad began to call me with increasing frequency as Mom's vascular dementia took over her personality, causing her to lose her memory and her temper more and more each day. When he called, he would recount what was happening to them, but he was strangely taciturn when it came to expressing how he felt about the barrage of anger my mom threw at him daily. This anger began to consume all their waking hours together. It was hard to comfort him with words alone; Dad was the kind of guy who liked to just sit and watch the ocean with a friend or loved one. He was not someone who would get all verbally mushy. He liked having someone physically close to him, he liked to talk, but he didn't like to talk about his feelings.

These calls from Dad as my mother declined made me want to be with my folks as they struggled with a disease that takes over whole families and has no cure. I came down to Los Angeles as often as I could to give Dad a break. But these short visits were ineffectual because, soon after I returned home to Seattle, any care plan I had worked on with Dad swiftly unraveled, and I would need to come back again a few weeks later for another visit that also had no lasting effect. Eventually, I realized that the only way I could be of help was to uproot my family from Seattle and move back home to be near both my parents. By then, Mom was in a facility where I went every day to spend time with her. At night, Dad often came over to our place for dinner. We went to the movies with him, and he took the girls out for frozen yogurt in the neighborhood. Dad liked to have me along when he ate meals with Mom. He would take her out someplace fun, like the Santa Monica pier. She could not really maintain a conversation anymore, but when we were all together, there was some feeling of normalcy.

Though we often had to deal with the logistics of Mom's care, my relationship with Dad was much as it had been when I was younger. We talked about books and movies and current events. We had deep philosophical conversations. Dad and I were at ease with each other and spoke about things that would be uncomfortable for most fathers and daughters; we even talked about death. My parents' advanced ages and medical conditions were not the only reasons we discussed this difficult subject. We had talked about death over the span of many years in the context of *The Tibetan Book of the Dead,* news articles about Jack Kevorkian, and the sad fact that his dear friend Bill Hayward had killed himself, as had Hayward's sister and mother. Even when I was back in high school we had talked about death: Carlos Castaneda's book *Journey to Ixtlan* had been required reading; Dad had read it with me, and we talked about the medicine man's role of taking drugs to understand death and help those who were alive prepare for it. Over the years, Dad had repeatedly said that hallucinogens had taken away any fear he ever had about dying, but that was not the sense I had back in that hospital room in Dallas.

After his death, I remained confused and unnerved by the way he had begged for forgiveness. What was he thinking of during that last long day? The easy answer was that he wanted to be forgiven for affairs he'd had while married to my mother. We only talked about these other women a few times as a family, taking our cue from Mom, who usually passed over the subject quickly. My brother probably knew more than the rest of us, but he just said, "Dad does his own thing," and he never went into detail.

Dad's lovers turned out in force to celebrate him at his memorials in Dallas and Los Angeles, according to new information I was getting from various sources just before and after he died. I began to wonder which women really were his lovers and which were just friends of the family. Did it matter? Mom always said Dad loved women. While we publicly said good-bye to our father, I tried to focus on all the wonderful things about my dad, but I couldn't help but be confronted with facts of his hidden life. Dad liked secrets. Secrets made him feel powerful and in control. Dad admired men who knew how to keep secrets and was especially enamored with a Texan who had a lot of them, oil tycoon H. L. Hunt. Dad was very impressed that after Hunt died, the public learned that he had more than one secret family and fourteen children.

Dad made a game of keeping his mistresses' identities unknown. It was like a game we played with him when we were kids. It was a treasure-hunt game he called Hide in Plain Sight. He would show us an object and make us leave the room. Then he would hide the object, not under something, not hidden from view, but somewhere that you might not notice, as though it were in plain sight. We would come back in the room and hunt for the object, and it sometimes took quite a while. Dad was good at camouflaging things; he understood what people noticed and what they didn't. I think Dad had lovers like this—people we all knew, people who were a part of our lives who regularly had dinner with the family but were also his special intimate friends. Memorials are often the place where secrets come out. The woman who had crawled into his bed at the hospital on his last day did not call attention to herself, though she was present at two of the three public memorials. She was very respectful, but another woman at the memorial in LA grabbed both my arms and demanded my full attention. She made a point of telling me that being with my father for years in Santa Fe had been the greatest experience of her life. I blinked for a moment trying to get my bearings. Who was she? What did she mean to my father? Was she his mistress?

Looking into her eyes, I immediately remembered that she was a journalist I'd met years ago when I was on her talk show. Her show had featured my paintings when they were on display at an art opening in LA in the mid-1980s. As I recalled, she had been an unusually astute interviewer who asked well-informed questions about my grandmother, Dad, and me. What I did not know at the time was that she had gotten all her information from Dad because she had been an intimate friend of his; how intimate I will never know.

I recalled the only other time I had encountered her. It happened one morning long after my art show, when she had emerged from one of the many bedrooms at Dad's giant home in Ojai. No one bothered to introduce us, and it took me a while to figure out who she was because she looked so different from the formal interviewer I had met years ago. She was wearing one of the Jacuzzi robes my mom designed and created. She sat at the breakfast table with all of us, including Mom and the grandkids, as if she were a part of the family, and we talked about the Internet. I remember that she spoke fast and confidently, seemingly eager to display her knowledge.

I suppose I always sensed that my father had many women in his life besides my mother, but I never asked about them. So it was disconcerting, at best, to have the blinders lifted from my eyes right after he died as I was forced to recognize what these women might have been to him. It was a shock to learn that the journalist was likely not the only one of them who had been guests in our home. Yet I had managed to remain naïvely unaware of their intimacy with my dad. All I had known was that they had been nice to me. There were all these women who helped me with my acting career or promoting my artwork. When he was alive, I really had not wanted to know which women were his lovers and which were just family friends. But then on the night of the memorial in LA, I had to confront this woman's intensity of the emotion and her relationship with my father, whatever that relationship might have been, and do so at a time when my grief was new and profound. Thankfully, I was surrounded by family and friends, with the conspicuous and regrettable exception of my mother, who was too far gone to attend.

With Mom conveniently out of the way, this former journalist and talk show host was not the only woman in attendance at the memorial who would go to some lengths to tell me that Dad was the most important man in her life. I was amazed that none of them were sympathetic enough to realize that these were not words I wanted or needed to hear right at that moment. In any case, I simply told each of them, as quietly and dismissively as possible, that many people loved my dad and felt that spending time with him was the best thing that had ever happened to them. This was the truth; these women were not the only ones who felt his loss deeply.

The memorials were populated by scores of people whose lives my father had touched. There was a woman a few years younger than I who had had a troubled childhood and had called regularly to talk with Dad since the early 1970s. He had long, long talks with her on and off for more than forty years. He had even put me on the phone with her sometimes to talk to her and comfort her, thinking a teen would understand another teen best.

There were people Dad had given money to when they'd been in tough spots and artists whose work he'd championed and single mothers, with their now-grown children by their side, standing before the microphone telling the crowd about how he had supported them and had been the person whom they had been able to confide in when they felt all alone. Dad had been the man in their lives. Dad's whole motorcycling gang came in full regalia. His professional friends came, all sorts of people who had worked with him over the years. As testament to the deep friendships my father maintained, his two best friends, whom he had been close to for over sixty years, came and spoke. Roger had been his high school roommate, and Henri was the man who had introduced my parents to each other and had been the best man at their wedding.

All the stories I have heard since Dad died helped me understand what a rich and complicated life he led. The thing I could not understand was why he was asking for forgiveness.

If I were to decide he was asking forgiveness for fooling around, I'd be giving myself a neat and tidy way of wrapping things up and walking away. But I didn't want to walk away. Throughout my life, I had looked the other way when it came to anything that might take my dad off his pedestal. But now I didn't want a godlike dad; I just wanted to understand him. And so I embarked on a search to discover who my dad had been.

Memory can be slippery. How you remember something can be far more important than what actually happened when it comes to the formation of your emotional structure and the way you think. As I embarked on my search to understand what had tormented my father in his last hours, I was interested in finding out as much as I possibly could and getting the other people's memories to corroborate my own. I unearthed and read twenty diaries I had kept over the years; I was surprised to find that I had started writing them as early as the age of ten. I found boxes of VHS tapes of all sorts of family events, including my first wedding and holiday dinners and the opening of an art exhibition that Dad had attended wearing a brown cowboy hat that matched his favorite hunting/fishing jacket that I had custom painted for him (it was covered with images of jumping trout with a bird of prey on the back). I wondered how I would be able to view this obsolete form of recorded personal history until a dear friend lent me an old VHS player she had in her garage. My family came alive for me again as I watched hours of home movies and dozens of talk shows that my father had taped whenever anyone in our family was interviewed. Viewing them, I experienced the embarrassment that anyone feels when seeing his or her awkward younger self, especially because many of the videos were of interview shows, *The Merv Griffin Show*, *Oprah*, and *Good Morning America*. Loads of people had seen me making a fool of myself when I was a nervous twentysomething trying hard to please everyone. The way I had looked and behaved made me cringe. The most embarrassing of all these shows was the episode of *Oprah* in which I was interviewed along with several other children of Hollywood stars. That particular interview had taken place at a terrible point in my life. I was a wreck; my goals and self-image were in flux. A series of events had recently lead me to quit acting, starting with being told by a casting director, at an audition, that he had seen a nude picture of me in *Vogue*, and ending with a well-meaning director pushing me past my emotional comfort zone in order to get a good performance out of me. It was a point in my life when I wanted to leave Hollywood far behind: I'd gotten married, and in so doing, I changed my name. I was trying to reinvent myself by moving away from my family and settling in New Mexico, and yet there I was, back on TV because my father encouraged me to do it. On this particular show, I sported an unflattering mullet hairstyle and wore an oversized suit with giant '80s shoulder pads that was designed to completely hide my body. Oprah was kind and used all her skill to put this group of nervous celebrity offspring at ease, but of all the young people on stage, I was especially awkward, and by the time the show ended, my accent had changed from British to California girl to Texan. This accent switching was a trait I found my grandma and Dad were also prone to in many of their interviews, but on them, it sounded good.

I also watched a video of a show that had taken place a few years later and made up for those first clumsy attempts to present myself to the public. This time, I was not being interviewed as J. R.'s daughter; instead, my whole family was in attendance at one of my first big art exhibits. Their love for me flowed out of the television. Now in my fifties, I saw the young woman I once was with new eyes: there I was interacting with my parents and grandmother in a place where I was truly comfortable. I could see that I was very happy that day, but my happiness was even more profound all these years later as I heard my family praising my early work as an artist. Clearly, a shift in my perspective has taken place. I understand family better now and know what it feels like to be a proud parent. The look of love and pride that I saw on my father's face is a look I know very well now that I've experienced the feelings that occasion it. My dad must have been feeling the same pride I feel for my daughters as I witness them growing into their wonderful adult selves.

My dad and my grandma were good at telling stories that people loved to hear because they were pros. My grandma, the musical comedy actress Mary Martin, was a Broadway legend, and as the cameras rolled, she said, in her perfect theatrical diction, "I am proud to be in my granddaughter's show."

You could see that she loved being interviewed, and she happily went on to explain what she meant. She told a funny story about taking me shopping when I was about six years old. Apparently, I stopped her in the street and said, "Someday, if you are very good, I will let you be in one of my shows."

Back then, we both thought that being in a show meant being

in the theater, but I had left the family business and was no longer an actress. My show was in an art gallery, and it had sold out and been well reviewed in the *Los Angeles Times*. I had worked hard to make the best paintings I could, but I was never under any illusion that the television crews were there to shine a spotlight on me as an emerging painter. I knew that I was in the limelight by association, but it was the light in my parents' eyes that made the evening one of the happiest in my memory.

The videos made me miss my family very much. I missed my grandmother, who always let everyone know that she was the most important person in the room while at the same time making me feel like the most important person in the world to her. I missed my father's hugs and the playful way his laughter bubbled out of him. I missed my mother's smile, and watching her when she was young had left me with the longing to be with the strong, vibrant person she had once been.

As I watched these many tapes, the picture of my family's life together became richer and sharper. I often felt I had been transported back in time in order to make sense of events and of people who, in real time, I had simply experienced. Dad, as he appeared in the videos, had no relation at all to the person he was in his final hours. And so, after watching these glimpses of life as it had been, I sought out many people whose lives Dad had touched in the hope of understanding why a seemingly happy, contented man who never apologized for anything during his life had begged for forgiveness when he was dying.

I Googled him repeatedly, and each time I did, I'd discover new things had been posted that weren't there the day before. I found: Larry Hagman memorial . . . Larry Hagman and marijuana . . . and LSD . . . and *Dallas* . . . Larry Hagman and organ donors, Larry Hagman as

Tony Nelson, kissing Jeannie on *I Dream of Jeannie* . . . registering with the Peace and Freedom Party . . . supporting renewable energy . . .

At one point, my search revealed 1,270,000 results about Dad. Many of the things I learned about him were familiar to me, but his interview in *The Guardian* on September 8, 2012, titled "My Family Values," gave me a perspective on his thinking that I had not known. He spoke about the pain of coming from a broken home. When the interviewer asked what he wanted to teach his children, he said, "I have taught my own children to be as truthful as possible and to be kind. I am glad I have had such a long marriage—I wanted to give my children a stable start in life, but it hasn't made much difference to them. My son has been married three times; my daughter twice." This statement stung and surprised me as well: he had never said that he was disappointed in us because we had both been divorced. Yet his response to this interviewer made it clear that he thought we had failed. Though I did not like to be criticized, upon reflection I realized he *had* taught me to be truthful and kind. All this information, old and new, and the emotions it elicited would, at times, become overwhelming, but it also helped me make sense of my life in ways that had always eluded me.

I reread Dad's official autobiography and some unofficial ones; I sent away for *The Larry Hagman Handbook* thinking it might contain some things I didn't already know. But it had no surprises, and anyway, it was just a collection of facts, and as Norman Mailer once said, "Facts are nothing without their nuance."

Still, seeing dates of shows Dad had done did bring back memories, like the time we were all at a resort dinner theater in Michigan while Dad was in a play called *The Golden Fleecing*. We had lived there all summer, and my brother and I had made the hotel lobby our playground.

Looking at Dad's TV history, I remembered being on the set of the short-lived series *Here We Go Again* on a day when Mom brought a camp stove with her and made vegetarian stir-fry for Dad on the back lot. Dad was on a health kick, and food services were not interested in accommodating a vegetarian diet back in those days, so Mom stepped in and made him exactly what he wanted; it was just one of the countless things she did to encourage him and keep him well and happy.

There were so many things that I remembered. These memories were like images on a kaleidoscope, one shifting into the next with no apparent pattern or meaning. Dad was not an easy man to understand; he was so full of contradictions. He'd polish off a bottle or two of wine and then go to skid row in downtown Los Angeles, pull drunks off the street, and take them to sober up at the Midnight Mission. He didn't mind being called a pothead, but he refused to think of himself as a drunk. "I only drink wine and beer," he'd say. "That's not really drinking."

He never likened the way he drank to the way his much-despised stepfather did, which was to drink huge tumblers of gin, pretending it was water. Dad prided himself on not being at all like his stepfather, Richard, whose addictions had colored all his attitudes, including—and maybe especially—the totally negative way in which he interacted with Dad. Still, the amount of wine drank in our house was astounding—at least several bottles a day. While I was growing up, the store I shopped in most often with Dad was the liquor store. He had many drinking buddies; the era of the two-martini lunch was not yet gone. All Dad's friends drank a lot. An example of their ethos was displayed in his good friend Carroll O'Connor's kitchen where a sign read, "Wine kills slowly, and I am not in a hurry."

To Dad, drunks were people who passed out on city streets; he couldn't have a drinking problem, he reasoned, because he drank socially, on his penthouse balcony in Santa Monica, hanging out with friends while watching the sunset over the Pacific Ocean. Drunks did not live such charmed lives.

Dad's drinking seldom caused him to have a temper, though sometimes he could be cuttingly sarcastic and stern. In most of my memories, he was a nurturing, reassuring, and loving father who patiently taught me how to whistle, how to ride a bike, and how to tie my shoes; he also taught me how to behave in the wilderness when we were out hunting. I had to stand perfectly silent and still as he aimed and then shot his prey; at other times, he would point in a direction, and I had to run like hell to get away from some hypothetical danger he had sighted to teach me survival skills and obedience.

He taught me so much about the world; he took me everywhere with him, even places I did not really belong. In the 1960s, people did not bring their kids to cocktail parties, but that did not stop Dad. I am sure there were plenty of hosts who raised their eyebrows when the Hagmans marched into posh Beverly Hills parties like a pair of ducks with their ducklings in tow. Mom and Dad brought my brother and me along never thinking about whether it would be fun for us; his attitude was that we were a family, and families did things together. I remember studying the interiors of these grand Beverly Hills homes, looking at the way people dressed, and hearing the cadence of their conversation and the clinking of their glasses.

On the other end of the spectrum, he took me to love-ins and peace rallies that were such a vital part of the LA scene when we arrived there in the '60s. Joints would be passed from hand to hand, and the music was very loud. People in flowing dress danced around like earthbound rainbows. I remember going to a Jimi Hendrix concert at a very early age and feeling like it was just a lot of disturbing noise. I begged Dad to take me home, but he told me that music history was being made and insisted we stay. He also took me to Watts where he was teaching acting and putting on a George Bernard Shaw play called *The Adventures of the Black Girl in Her Search for God*. He let me watch rehearsals, and I was a part of his class, though I was much younger than most people in it.

Later, in the early '80s, when *Dallas* was the most popular show on television, I often visited him on location. This was during the country-western dance craze, and when Larry Hagman and Linda Gray showed up at a club accompanied by their entourages, everyone made way for us. I learned the Texas two-step and went riding on the mechanical bull. Later that year, with Dad having achieved worldwide status as the man people "loved to hate," the whole family was invited to take a transatlantic trip on the ocean liner the *QE II*. We toured Europe, and on this trip, it seemed that all doors were opened to us. We were even invited to an elegant private tea with Princess Grace and her children at the royal palace in Monaco. Her Royal Highness made polite conversation, but the young prince and princess were more interested in a local soccer tournament than in meeting yet another famous person, and they were visibly bored. Three years later, after Princess Grace had died in a tragic car accident, we celebrated Prince Rainier's birthday with him at the Rockefeller compound on the Hudson river. The day was chilly and gray, so some of us sat around the fire after the birthday luncheon. The small group was lethargic, having drunk so many congratulatory toasts, and the conversation became dull. Dad wanted to make sure the prince was not bored this time, so he started throwing cash into the fireplace and, with a huge chuckle, watched as some of the richest people in the world tried to salvage the burning bills.

People come up to me all the time to tell me stories of how he impacted their lives. For instance, there was a woman in Weatherford, Texas, the small town where his mother was born, who called Dad to tell him she was about to lose the lease on the building in which she had a shop where she sold hand-painted clothes. Dad told her to paint a shirt depicting his internal organs, highlighting the new liver he had just received in his transplant surgery. She was to send it to him as fast as she could and to wait and see what would happen next. No questions asked, she did just what he told her to. That week, he wore the painted T-shirt while being interviewed on a national TV program. Suddenly, the woman was receiving countless orders from people all over the country requesting their own custom-painted T-shirts. The woman not only stayed in her shop, she now owns the building that houses it.

Throughout my life, I've met girls and women who would tell me my father had been like a father to them: from an early age, I knew full well I would never have exclusive rights to that feeling.

Dad kept in touch with an amazing number of people, and he liked having lots of people around. He was generous and always outgoing and loved to see the amazed look on someone's face when he quietly doled out some cash without expecting to get anything back.

He was a grown man who would play, dance, sing, drink, and get high. He was always so much fun to be with. I could understand why, in the months after he passed, I got at least one call a day from someone who would tell me, "He was my best friend," or "I had the best experience of my life with your dad," or "Your home was the most welcoming place I have ever been in."

So many people loved my dad. But I don't think any of them knew him any better than I did.

He had a tremendous presence, and you always knew when he was in the room. It was as if he had his own energy field around him; he would be smiling and had a booming, infectious laugh. Justin Fonda, Peter's son, called Dad the biggest man in the world, and few would disagree; though at six foot one he was not the tallest man, he made himself larger by entering a gathering wearing wild, colorful clothes, and visuals alone were not enough: often, he would interject some kind of tune, either playing music loudly on his stereo or, if that were not an option, he would play his flute or whistle or sing.

In order to guarantee that every day was filled with fun activities, he always carried a big bag filled with all sorts of toys, among them a flute, a Frisbee, a Swiss Army knife with corkscrew attached, a kaleidoscope. He played Frisbee everywhere and said he once threw it around with people who had been waiting for hours in line to view Lenin's tomb in Moscow's Red Square as the severe-looking authorities watched. At least that is the story he told me when he returned, but then Dad loved a good story, so I don't know for a fact that he actually did what he said he did; you could never be sure with Dad!

I do know for a fact that, in addition to his fun props, he always carried his mini, portable, battery-powered fan and his bubble bear, which he employed whenever he was around someone smoking cigarettes; he would squeeze the bubble bear's tummy so a wand would emerge, and then he'd blow bubbles at the smokers in his vicinity, in that way annoying them as much as their smoke was annoying him. Perhaps one of the more unusual things he insisted on carrying around each day was the string hammock that he stored at the bottom of his big bag. He kept it with him because he had once gotten stuck overnight in an airport, and he was determined that he would have a comfortable place to sleep if it ever happened again.

One of the things that made this forensic search for Dad so difficult was that he was such a good bullshitter. He was so good at making things up that I never knew what was real and true and what was not.

For instance, we had countless discussions about the things he read; he was a voracious reader who subscribed to dozens of magazines.

I loved these conversations, yet I could never be sure if what he was saying was something he'd learned or something he'd made up. He would go on about how nuclear reactors worked and about how, when crates of shoes fell off boats in the ocean, the currents brought only left shoes to the coastal beaches of California. When I repeated the "facts" I had learned from my father to other people, I often found that his information was more entertaining than valid, though there were also many times when his eccentric opinions proved to be astoundingly right on. I learned to preface anything he said to me that I passed on to others with the following disclaimer: "According to Dad . . ."

My father always seemed accessible and open, but that was a delusion. He kept so many of his feelings to himself; in the ways that matter most, he was elusive and, in addition, he was a chameleon who, when he was in Texas, would sound as Southern as Willie Nelson, just as he'd sound more British than Noël Coward after two days in London.

Everyone who met him had their own particular view of him. Wealthy, conservative Texas oilmen felt he really *was* his character on

Dallas and therefore was just like them, but environmentalists knew he was an ally in their fight against global warming. There is a photo that my mom took of Nancy Reagan sitting on my dad's lap when he played J. R./Santa Claus at Ronald Reagan's White House, wearing a red Santa suit and bright-red Stetson hat, but though he supported a Reagan on his knee, his political support was firmly and unapologetically with more radical groups like the Peace and Freedom Party. People who confused Dad with the character he famously played did not read the extensive interviews he gave that detailed his political views and constant drug use.

Despite his many affairs, he never dreamed of divorcing my mother and always made a point of talking about his stable marriage. His successful marriage was one of the aspects of his life that he wanted to be known for; to him, it meant that—in his real life—he wasn't like J. R.

Dad presented different sides of himself to every person he encountered; he had a multifaceted personality. He also had an uncanny ability to sense exactly what a person wanted him to be, and he would find that person inside himself and then do his chameleon act by becoming his companion's ideal fantasy of Larry Hagman, which ranged from cutthroat Texas businessman to peacenik hippie to, in one particular instance, a genuine Prince Charming. That happened when he met the matriarch of the Hormel meatpacking business at her mansion in Bel Air. Dad sized her up and found the perfect way to flatter her. She was tiny in stature, but despite her size, she had a commanding presence that demanded the respect of her many sons and their extended families. But Dad sensed a deep sadness in her and figured that her outward stance masked a desire to be feminine. He guessed that since her husband had died, no one had courted her and that the flirtatious young French girl she had once been was just below the surface, longing to be recognized. He had my mother search high and low for a pair of "glass slippers." Mom always carried out his wishes, and she found a perfect size-five pair of Lucite pumps. The next time he was invited to Madame Hormel's home, Dad arrived dressed in a suit. As soon as he entered the room where she was seated, he bent down next to her, and, though she pretended to protest, he took off her shoes and tickled her toes. He then produced two glass slippers from his pockets and slipped them onto her beautifully manicured feet. He asked her to walk around the room while wearing those glass slippers, and as she did so, he watched her intently, all the while exclaiming that she had great legs! As soon as she sat down, he was kneeling at her side again; he removed one of the shoes, poured cham-pagne into it, and drank it and then declared that the drink had been transformed into the most divine ambrosia by her dainty foot.

It seemed that everyone who knew him had their own precise notions of who he was: to his neighbors at the beach, he was the Mad Monk of Malibu who wore the distinctive "monk's robes" Mom had designed and made for him to wear as he led flag parades at sunset along the water's edge; to his stoner buddies, he was a student of life seeking to answer the big questions of existence by dropping acid; to his motorcycle gang, he was a loyal member who knew and adhered to all the secret protocols and codes of behavior while on group rides all over the country; to people who ran into him at the liquor store, he might be that weird guy dressed in a yellow chicken suit. He loved to surprise people, and he was always on the lookout for new costumes—some of them incredibly garish, like his chicken suit—and all of them designed to make sure he turned heads and attracted attention every-where he went.

While researching Dad, I came upon a story posted on Facebook by Oscar Hammerstein's grandson, who was reminiscing publicly about going to an amusement park as a little kid with both our fathers. We were still living in New York at the time, and Palisades Park was the run-down amusement park near New York City that became famous as a place to go when you were high. I don't remember it well, but according to Andy, when Dad took us to the park, he had dressed in overalls, without a shirt underneath, all the while chewing a piece of hay and pretending to be a country bumpkin on his first adventure in the big city, talking with a thick accent while scratching his head and saying, "Aw, gee whiz" at the end of every ride like the character Jethro from *The Beverly Hillbillies*. Dad had the discipline to stay in character for hours. His antics left a lasting impression on a young boy. Andy thought Dad was "really out there," which I thought was telling coming from a guy who came from four generations of theater people and must have known a lot of wild actors.

I lived with Dad's shenanigans every day, so they were normal for me; it was only when I read about him from other people's perspectives that I could see how kooky he appeared to many people. I read about one incident in a book by one of President Clinton's assistants— Melinda Bates, who took Dad on a VIP tour of the White House. Dad appeared appropriately dressed for his role of Very Important Person, wearing a sedate and well-tailored Brooks Brothers' suit. But as they stopped and leaned forward to look at a painting, she noticed something odd about his attire.

"What an unusual tie," she said. "I can't quite make out the design."

Dad could not suppress a gleeful smile. "It's ducks fucking," he said.

My relationship to my dad was both warm and puzzling: Like the fictional character J. R., who lived under the same roof with his entire extended family, Dad often stated that "family comes first." As his daughter, I was truly close to him, and we spent a lot of time together. We spoke on the phone regularly no matter where in the world either of us might be and always kept each other apprised about what was going on in our lives, yet there were many aspects of his life that made me uncomfortable. When I got to a certain age, I intentionally chose not to do certain things with him, like smoke pot or take hallucinogens or go to hippie festivals. I avoided him when he was drunk and when he was paying attention to the numerous women who sought him out. But after his tumultuous last hours, I felt that I had to look at all these aspects of his life because they might help me make sense of who he was and who I was to him.

The frantic way he'd asked for forgiveness on his deathbed was so unlike anything I'd ever experienced him doing. Those words and his desperation haunted me; because I needed to understand what he had been trying to tell me, I would have to remember everything I could. Maybe if I could remember enough, I would find the clues that would help me understand why he had asked to be forgiven.

3
—

Pot and Friends to Share It

I HARDLY EVER SAW my father when he wasn't stoned or cruising on wine.

I don't think I ever knew him sober except for a brief period just before and just after his liver transplant, which had become necessary after he was diagnosed with alcohol-induced cirrhosis of the liver.

Dad might have been even more of a drinker if he hadn't met Jack Nicholson, who turned him onto pot, the substance he fell permanently in love with.

The pot adventure began in a tropical paradise. The year was 1964, and I was just six years old. Dad had brought all of us on location with him in Acapulco, Mexico, where he was making a movie called *Ensign Pulver*. This was great for Mom, who had been working day and night making one-of-a-kind gowns for her very demanding clients. Dad had promised her some much-needed leisure time while we were in Mexico, and to make that possible, we brought our babysitter, Peggy, from New York. Peggy was amazed by this good fortune because she had not traveled much in her life except between Ireland, where she was raised, and the poor Irish neighborhood in New York City where she was living at the time.

One of the best parts of this trip was that we were going to stay at the Hilton. We had heard a lot about Hilton Hotels from a good family friend who was a Hilton executive. We could hardly believe that we were going to get to stay in one of these beautiful modern places he had described. Peggy could not stop talking about the luxury of sleeping in the Hilton's ice-blue sheets and having use of the big fluffy towels that a maid would change for her every day.

The hotel pool was huge and had an island in the middle where fruity cocktails were made and then poured into coconut shells embellished with little umbrellas; you drank them as you swam. My baby brother and I spent our days at the pool with Peggy. During the heat of the day, Dad and everyone on the set were boiling in the sun, since they were filming on the deck of a naval ship, but when their workday was over, the pool quickly filled with the rowdy, playful men who made up the cast. Before you knew it, everyone was wildly drunk. We watched in amazement as one of the stuntmen climbed up the outside of the hotel from balcony to balcony until he got to the roof. The guys were a lot of fun, and a bunch of them taught me how to dive off the high-diving board. I vaguely remember Jack Nicholson, who played one of the leads in the film, but whenever I saw him, he seemed to smile all the time. Much later, when I was working as a young actress in Los Angeles, I met him and his then partner Angelica Huston several times at his home and out on the town at a roller disco place that he frequented in the early '80s. But I did not know how much Dad's fellow actor had changed his life until I read Dad's autobiography, *Hello Darlin'*, in which Dad detailed his first encounter with marijuana. Jack decided it was time to introduce my dad to pot after seeing him get drunk one too many times at lunch. After a few tokes on the joint, Dad told Jack he'd rather have a martini because he didn't feel anything and asked him when the pot would kick in. With his ever-present grin, Jack told my dad that he had asked that same question twelve times already. It must have been right about then that Dad developed a grin as ever present and bright as Jack's. The smile looked different on my dad, but once he found it, he never lost it. I have boxes and boxes of photographs, and the smile is on his face in almost every single one. Dad looked like the happiest man in the world after that day in Mexico. He began to relax; he savored the substance he had taken in and recognized its ability to brighten his attitude and his life. And, on the day of his first high, he liked the feeling so much that he went right out of the room and found my mom so he could share it with her. They stayed high all day. In fact, my folks got so stoned that they did not even feel the 7.4-magnitude earthquake that rocked Acapulco.

From Dad's point of view, he had discovered pot at just the right time. The drug helped him segue into the life he was just beginning in California and into the alternative lifestyle of the 1960s that he found in LA and which suited him perfectly. He loved the hippie look: he grew a moustache; he wore flowery peasant shirts and bought his first pair of what became his signature rose-colored glasses. His mantra was and always would be: DON'T WORRY! BE HAPPY! FEEL GOOD! Those six words meant so much to him that my mother had them etched on his bathroom mirror.

Dad was a good networker before the phrase was invented. He connected with all the people he worked with back east, and one of them was Brandon de Wilde, whom Dad had worked with in the theater and with whom he had just finished the movie *In Harm's Way*. Brandon was eleven years younger than Dad and had made enough money to buy a house with some land around it in Topanga Canyon. The stoned and laid-back vibe at that house was so different from the far more uptight atmosphere we'd experienced while staying with friends of the family in their grand country houses in Connecticut. Those homes had manicured lawns for playing civilized games like croquet, but the scruffy California landscape was wild and untamed. Topanga is still much as it was in those early days of the hippie movement, with shops selling tie-dyed clothes and handcrafted leather goods, and lots of vegetarian restaurants and colorful flags flying. To get to Topanga, you drive east from Malibu along the Pacific Coast Highway for a few miles and then take a winding road up into a canyon that rises high above the ocean. The topography makes the place feel like you are getting out of town even though it is less than an hour from Hollywood. Whenever I drive through Topanga Canyon, I always find myself thinking of our visits to the de Wilde home when I was a child. Brandon's wife was a good friend of Susan Fonda, Peter Fonda's wife. Susan vividly remembers the day that she walked into the de Wildes' living room and found Dad, who was on his first acid trip with his trip "guide" Larry Hall, who had just given my dad a little "trip gift" to help him remember the experience. It was a mother-of-pearl muscle shell that had a hinge and a clasp on it so it functioned as a lovely little box.

Though Dad had met Peter in New York several years before, it was not until Susan got together with my mother that our families truly bonded; when they became reacquainted, Dad had just recently worked with Peter's father, Henry Fonda, on a movie. The two men became lifelong friends, and they had a lot to talk about since Dad's mother, the musical comedy star Mary Martin, was as famous on

Broadway as Peter's dad was in the world of films. And Mary and Henry had something in common outside the sphere of performing, for—though few people know this—both were avid and talented painters.

Our two families spent a lot of time together. I always think of the Fonda kids, Bridget and Justin, as my younger siblings once removed.

When Susan and I were reminiscing together about this time in our lives, we both recalled spending a lot of time at Brandon's place. Susan remembered him as a quiet man who spent a lot of time practicing guitar because he had a sincere desire to become a serious musician. I remember him surrounded by musicians, and the details of one particular party at his house remain as clear to me as the shell box "trip gift" is to Susan. It was a sunny day, and we were playing outdoors, painting a mural on the high walls of the handball court. As night fell, we stayed on. It was then that some wonderful musicians like David Crosby started showing up with their instruments and began playing their brand of folksy rock. Those who didn't know how to play pounded on drums or danced. I was that awkward age when I no longer was one of the younger children present, but I was still a long way from being an adult. The euphoria of the crowd was in some ways like the gatherings of theater people who had hung out at my parents' apartment when we lived in New York. But the mood was different: it was younger, druggier, more raucous, and as the night wore on, though I was so tired I could barely keep my eyes open, I became transfixed by the slender women with long straight hair dancing to the live music while wearing short go-go dresses that looked like sexy, shiny chain mail and were ingeniously constructed out of the flip tabs from the many cans of beer. The dancing took on an even more dreamlike quality as I watched through the smoke haze, pot mixed with cigarettes, and the stoned onlookers pointed the newly invented handheld laser lights at the dancers, causing the strong red light to flash on and off, illuminating the undulating women. It was like being in a movie, and I must have been stoned too, given the fact that I was surrounded by all that pot smoke. And I was fascinated: these women were beautiful; they redefined my idea of how grown women should look and behave. They were so different from the more conventional grown women I knew back home in New York. Lost in the rhythm and caught up in the group euphoria, I joined the dancers and must have looked pretty funny—a chubby little girl trying to emulate the go-go dancers' style, gyrating my hips and shimmying my nonexistent chest, but dancing was pure joy to me. My own kids have seen me dance so many times that they have gotten over being embarrassed by their middle-aged mother who still moves to the music whenever possible. Time has not changed the little girl inside me who learned to dance with wild abandon at Brandon de Wilde's hippie palace in the Topanga hills. Dad loved the relaxed energy of his young friends, and it was a relief for him not to have to struggle to fit in as he had with his mother's older, sophisticated New York crowd. Gone were the formal dinners and nightclubs, and in their place were the energy of youth and folk rock music and new perspectives on everything under the sun.

Brandon and his easygoing lifestyle really appealed to Dad, who said he too wanted a home where people could come to play and make music and be themselves. Sadly, that friendship ended a few years after that memorable party. Brandon died in a car accident at the age of thirty and, like James Dean and Marilyn Monroe, will be eternally young and hauntingly beautiful.

Dad's drug taking was a huge part of his search for some kind of spiritual life that would not restrict his behavior but would instead set him free. He wanted to break all the rules he had been taught as a child and find a new way of living.

In pursuit of this new life, in addition to registering with the Peace and Freedom Party, he read Alan Watts's *The Joyous Cosmology*; he read the *Whole Earth Catalog, Siddhartha,* and *The Urantia Book.* He listened to Jimi Hendrix and Bob Dylan; I was with him when he had drinks with his fellow Southerner Janis Joplin at his favorite hangout on Sunset Boulevard. All his life, Dad had the habit of finding a restaurant where his friends would know they could find him on a given day or time, and for many years that place was a Chinese restaurant with a beautiful courtyard protected from the busy boulevard by a high wall. For years, even long after he had finished his work in the hit TV show *I Dream of Jeannie,* Dad held court at Mr. Luck's restaurant for late lunches on Friday or Saturday. He would sit at a big, round table with a lazy Susan in the middle that was constantly refilled with food, ordering bottle after bottle of Pouilly-Fuissé (he liked how the Chinese waiters pronounced the name of that wine). We never knew who would show up, though Peter Fonda and Bill Hayward were regulars.

Over lunch, they talked about all the news of the day, and at one point, the Fondas, both Peter and Jane, became convinced they were on some kind of government surveillance list, and Dad figured he must be on that list too. I think the prospect of it truly excited him. He marched for civil rights and campaigned to have minorities on his show. He was a regular at the happenings of the era, among them peace rallies and music festivals.

One lasting image I have of him was formed in my late teens when I went with some friends to a Grateful Dead concert. I was dancing to the music when I felt someone's eyes on me. I looked up and saw Dad standing some thirty feet away. He was looking at me lovingly; he loved to see me dance. He didn't seem like a parent in that crowd. He just seemed like another Deadhead. I could tell from the grin on his face that he was totally stoned.

He so completely embraced the sex, drugs, and rock-and-roll ethos of the era that he lived it to the end of his days. When he died at the age of eighty-one, his refrigerator was packed with marijuana brownies.

My first experience with pot came when I was eight years old and found a batch of brownies that had been hidden away. I thought my mom was trying to keep the sweets away from me because she had me on another one of her diets; she and Dad were always trying to get me to lose some weight. As soon as I found them, I jammed two of them in my mouth and gulped them down before anyone could see me. Pretty soon I was very high and confused. I remember feeling very emotional. I began sobbing uncontrollably about my grandpapa Ben who had just died a few days before, and the next minute I was falling over with laughter at stuff I saw on TV. There was a new dance called the Pony, and I began prancing around. Next, I became mesmerized watching James Brown wailing and contorting as he sang. At some point, I must have passed out because that is all I can remember. The next day, Mom and Dad explained what had happened to me, and I was frightened of pot after that. I would stand with the grown-ups when they formed circles to pass joints around, but I always passed the roach on without toking on it. When I was in high school, every-one in my peer group smoked pot, but I never liked the feeling of being out of control, and by the time I got to college, I had pretty much phased marijuana out of my life.

Dad never pushed me to join him, but I knew he thought I was a square; he teased me about it in front of his friends. He could not understand why I wouldn't want to mellow out and be part of the fun. Occasionally, in adulthood, I tried to drink with him. I like having a glass of wine at the end of the day while talking with good friends over a meal, but more than two glasses of wine and I know I am unsafe to manage a car or, for that matter, make good decisions. When smoking pot, I felt even more intensely out of control, and I did not want to be that way around him and his buddies.

But after he died, I felt I might have been too critical, too uptight. He had resented it when I tried to encourage him to not indulge by refusing to drink or smoke with him. As a result, I had missed out on being with him on many occasions, missed having fun with him, and, at times, I had lost his trust because he saw me as judgmental. It's probably not possible—or at least not likely—for a child of any age to influence a parent to change his or her behavior in ways that could make him or her healthier. As time went on, I knew that Dad's continued drinking and drugging would compromise his fragile immune system, and it was hard to watch him hurt himself. I talked to therapists and went to Al-Anon meetings where I was encouraged not to be an enabler and to voice my concerns about his drinking. I did that, but the only result was that it just pissed him off. I went to a few AA meetings, and the takeaway from them was that I could have little or no influence on whether he drank to excess or not; my father was the only person who had any control over his drinking habits.

When he was gone, I wondered if we might have been closer

throughout his life if I had just kept my mouth shut. I wanted to experience a connection with him, so I sought out some of his pot-smoking friends whom he thought of as family. Dad had so many friends. I admired his ability to just hang out. I always need to be doing something, cleaning house or making a painting or cooking, as if my world would fall apart if I weren't working. But Dad lived like he had all the time in the world to play. His Santa Monica friends met once a week in an old Victorian-style beach shack one block from the sand where they played poker and smoked pot and ate huge, delicious home-cooked meals and told stories and laughed a lot. Even as my mom became more out of it as her Alzheimer's disease progressed, Dad still brought her along, and everyone made her feel comfortable and welcome.

I went with Dad a few times and met his friends, who were quite a diverse group: there was a lawyer, a retired flight attendant, a jeweler, some lovely ladies, and a warm, jolly, white-bearded guy who must have been quite a looker on his motorcycle a decade or two earlier. On my forays into their world, I would savor the aromas of the feast to come—roast chicken with all the fixings or herb-encrusted salmon—but I never stayed long. The haze of dope made me uncomfortable even though I liked his friends and was always grateful he had kind people who supported him and fed him, especially after Mom was too far gone to be good company. He needed lots of companionship. He did not like to be alone.

One afternoon, a few months after Dad died, when my kids were away, I called an older married couple, some folks who were part of the group Dad played poker and smoked pot with every week. They had reached out to me at Dad's birthday party the year before. I had had a ball dancing with the husband, and they had both marveled at what a wild dancer I was and were surprised that I could be so much fun; I guessed that Dad had told them I was a stick in the mud. I was surprised when they welcomed me over the very same evening. The house was filled with the luscious scent of a Thanksgiving meal, though they hadn't been expecting me and there was no special occasion. Of course, they knew I didn't smoke; Dad had told them how not into it I was. I told them that I had been regretting not being more a part of Dad's life. I had been so busy keeping my kids on track with school and sports, and I had paid more attention to my mom in her decline than to Dad, who always seemed so happy. Now he was gone, and I missed him so much; I could see they did too. Could I try some pot? Could we get high together as a toast to the old man? If he knew somehow, he would get a chuckle out of it.

They were sweet and amused by my awkward handling of the joint they passed, and I took a sputtering toke while sitting on a step stool in their kitchen, where the walls were covered in memorabilia that looked like it had not been changed since the early 1960s. There were plates from world's fairs hung on the wall, pictures of motorcycles, and old photos of Muscle Beach, just down the street from where we were sitting, as it had looked in the old days. When they saw how quickly I got stoned, they kindly helped me to the couch, where they fed me. As I ate the delicious food, they talked to me in soft, reassuring tones about what a cool guy my dad was and how much fun they had playing poker and playing practical jokes on their friends together. We watched a Monty Python movie, and as I am an early-to-bed, early-to-rise kind of person, the wife could see I was getting tired, and so she suggested we walk on the beach together to make sure I was okay to drive. She was so kind to me. I think she wanted to give me some time alone with her in case I needed to talk about losing Dad. I would have liked to have talked about him, but I was still in the topsy-turvy stage of confusion that had set in when he died. I could not form any coherent words or thoughts about my feelings. I was simply relieved to be in the moment; being high, I felt very deeply the warmth of their kindness. All I could express was how glad I was that they had been so good to him and to my mom. Though I did not have much to say, the fresh air and the walk made me more alert.

I went home comforted.

After that evening, I had much more appreciation for the unusually supportive community with which Dad had surrounded himself. When you live with a famous person, you cannot help but be a bit cynical about the people he or she attracts. Most of these folks were, I believe, much like the couple who'd been so welcoming to me. These folks were not just hangers-on. They were not looking to bask in Dad's reflected glory but simply enjoying the light of his personality. Everyone was aware of his fame, but they were also part of the strange tribe that was like an extended family to him. I was grateful that they had been so kind to me in the depth of my sadness.

Over the years, I had come to demonize pot, feeling that the drug had come between my father and me. Smoking it made him forgetful and distant. Though I did not want to continue to indulge in the drug-induced intimacy, it was also true that smoking with Dad's friends allowed me to experience the communal quality that was one of the things that drew Dad to marijuana. Being with them, I had relaxed in their comfortable home. I had melted into their couch; my body had felt all soft, as if I had no bones. I giggled and did not feel my usual, burning need to do something. I was in the moment. My mind told me *be here now* like Baba Ram Dass wrote in the books Dad and I read together. Most of all, I had fun, and fun was what Dad was all about.

He made no apologies for his joyride through life. I know how hard he studied his script; he never went on set without knowing his lines, and he always rehearsed diligently. He was very disciplined, but somehow he always had time to party.

Growing up with my parents, I'd had a hard time keeping up with my schoolwork while all the drinking and dinner parties were going on all week. Participating in family dinners was too much fun. I was encouraged to stay and dance instead of going up to my room to focus on my studies. I was often tired at school, but Dad always seemed to have an amazing amount of energy. I know he did cocaine sometimes (his friends convinced me to rub some of it on my teeth when my braces hurt), but the type of energy Dad had was intrinsic to him. He had a natural dose of some special life force.

My brother and I often commented on it; even when we were in our twenties, Dad could stay up later, drink harder, and be ready to go to the next venue to keep dancing when we young folks were ready to pack it in. Dad would never be apologetic about doing drugs. That was obvious from the number of interviews he did discussing the beneficial properties of pot and LSD. He was comfortable with his drug use, and it was not what he would have been seeking forgiveness for.

Two days after getting high with Dad's friends, I went to their home and placed two dozen yellow roses on their doorstep. Whenever Dad was thanking someone or wanted to send something special for a birthday, he would give people the yellow roses of Texas.

The gesture was not lost on his friends and brought his spirit back to us all for a moment.

4

Two Stars

My FATHER'S MOTHER, Mary Martin, was a great, entrancing performer who became one of the most beloved entertainers of all time.

Mary had been only seventeen years old when Dad was born, but even at that early age, her drive to perform was unstoppable. Her passionate heart hardly skipped a beat after the birth of her baby boy, and soon she was dancing and singing again, with the complete support of her parents, who were behind her ambitions 100 percent. They even built Mary her own dance studio not far from her father's law office, where she taught tap and waltz and something that looked like ballet to local kids.

Meanwhile, Ben Hagman, who was Mary's husband and Dad's father, joined his father-in-law at his law practice. Preston Martin was one of the most well-respected lawyers in the community; as a sign of respect, people called him Judge Martin. He opened the doors of the legal profession for Ben, making the career the young man had dreamed of become reality. Grateful for the opportunity, Ben worked long hours all week—and, to let off steam, he went hunting with his drinking buddies almost every weekend.

The young couple barely saw each other, as Mary worked night and day at her dance school, which grew and grew. With his mother so consumed, the baby, named Larry but nicknamed Luke, was cared for by his grandmother and the nanny who had helped raise Mary.

Mary was only eighteen years old when she realized that, due to her limited knowledge of dance techniques, she needed to take classes herself to keep a step or two ahead of her growing roster of students. Enterprising young woman that she was, Mary found a dance-teacher training school in Los Angeles, California. Since Ben was working so hard, he did not object when Judge Martin, always completely devoted to his daughter's happiness, sent her off to dance and learn in Los Angeles. Mary's mother, Juanita, had given birth some years earlier to a boy who died in infancy, and she had yearned for a son since, so she was more than happy to keep little Luke at home with her.

Mary's solo trip showed her a glimpse of the life she wanted in the big, wide world. When she came back to Weatherford, she was restless. Ben loved the comforts of their small town, but Mary hungered for a more glamorous life in the city. I can only guess what the conversation was like in their home when Mary said she wanted to go back to LA for more dance lessons. Though I was quite young when Papa Ben died, I remember seeing my grandparents together and recognizing that he always had a soft spot for Mary, even long after their divorce. One year after her first trip to Los Angeles, she convinced her parents to send her back there. Given Ben's respect for Judge Martin and his appreciation of Mary's drive and talent, he did nothing to stand in her way. He may have been reassured that Mary would not get into trouble because this time, Grandma Juanita, baby Luke, and Mary's female companion Mildred Woods came along to see what Mary was up to in Los Angeles.

Mary's mother, Juanita, was a musician who had performed and taught violin at Weatherford College before her children were born. Though her own days in front of an audience were long gone, she was still a performer at heart, and so she was completely wrapped up in every aspect of Mary's career, and she wanted to see for herself what show business possibilities might be out there for her precious daughter.

In Los Angeles, all of them were inspired by the dream of sudden fame and stardom that attracted thousands of young, hopeful, Depression-era performers to Hollywood from small towns all over the United States. It was while Mary and her mother were in LA that it became obvious that Ben and Mary wanted entirely different kinds of lives; their divorce became inevitable and freed them both to pursue the lives they wanted.

So Mary began her real career as a performer, and she did so with Juanita always by her side caring for her precious Luke, her grandson and the baby boy she had wanted so much.

Having left Texas behind, Mary was working her way toward becoming one of the greatest stars of the American musical theater at a time when musical theater was at its peak of inventiveness, brilliance, and charm. Her success did not happen overnight; she auditioned tirelessly. Often she did not get the role, but her optimism and disarmingly open personality attracted many mentors and supporters, among them some notable millionaires. Winthrop Rockefeller gave her an incredible Indian raj necklace and matching earrings, both pieces festooned with emeralds, diamonds, and rubies. Stanley Marcus saw her at the night club at the Cine Grille on Hollywood Boulevard and sent her the perfect evening gown from his department store, saying he wanted to see her dressed properly when she performed at that venue.

Juanita wanted to protect Luke from Mary's flamboyant life as a single young woman, and for the most part, she did. She was surely a loving force in his life, but without a doubt, she was strict and gave him structure and guidance, sending him to kindergarten at the Black-Foxe Military Institute in LA.

Dad was five years old when Mary landed a role in *Leave It to Me!*, the Cole Porter show that would be her breakthrough. Dad and his grandmother took the train to New York to see her perform.

This was the show in which Mary sang "My Heart Belongs to Daddy" to the young Gene Kelly. For that number, she was dressed in a lynx coat and hat, and during the course of the song, she removed them, revealing that she was clad in nothing more than a pink satin lace chemise. She was a sensation and soon appeared on the cover of *Life* magazine, with a big centerfold spread of her doing her "striptease." Dad wrote about the experience of seeing her in the show. He said that he had been kind of embarrassed while also noting "by today's standards, her strip was not even a tease." In his memoir, he added that he never said anything to his mom about how uncomfortable he felt, instead telling her, "You've got great legs." This was not the kind of statement a child would make, but it is how he remembered the occasion.

It was during the run of that show, while singing "My Heart Belongs to Daddy" every night to great fanfare that Mary's father died.

She adored him but was not with him at the end; she would never miss a performance, not even to be at his side when he died.

After *Leave It to Me!*, Mary went back to LA to work in films and to be close to her newly widowed mother, who had moved there permanently with Luke.

I've often thought that if Juanita Martin had been able to pursue her own talent as a musician, it's possible that neither Mary nor Dad would have become the stars they did. But Juanita's own frustrations prompted her to transfer all her ambition to them.

As Mary's fame and reputation grew, Juanita stayed close to her, but not too close. She protected Mary from the demands and needs of her child just as she made sure that young Luke was protected from the frenetic whirl of Mary's suitors and the relentless demands of publicity appearances and performing. Still, Mary often turned to her for strength and encouragement. Juanita had a grounding effect on her irrepressible daughter.

But as Mary became more sophisticated, she grew out from under her mother's influence and sought out someone who had more showbiz savvy. She found someone who was equally devoted to making her successful and keeping her focused on her dreams as her loving parents always had. His name was Richard Halliday. As I learned later, Richard had always been looking for a talented person he could guide and even lead. Richard was all about control and perfection, and Mary, also a perfectionist, had always had someone in her life who took care of all the details and practicalities for her, and she was happy and relieved to cede control over real-life matters so that she could pour everything into her life on the stage.

I remember Richard well: he was tall and extremely thin, and everything about his style and manner suggested that he was gay. I believe they had more of a partnership than a marriage, but I know with certainty that he was totally devoted to her. Together they created one career that was much greater than careers that either of them would have been able to achieve individually. They were seen in the right places, wearing the right clothes, and together they worked day and night to choose the right theatrical properties to highlight Mary's exceptional talents.

In 1949, she became a sensation as Ensign Nellie Forbush in the original production of *South Pacific*. With that show, she became a muse for the great songwriting team of Richard Rodgers and Oscar Hammerstein and worked with them to create the role of Maria in one of their greatest hits, *The Sound of Music*.

The songs Mary sang in her favorite role as Peter Pan were composed by five people. The music was mostly by Mark "Moose" Charlap, with additional music by Jule Styne; most lyrics were written by Carolyn Leigh, with additional lyrics by the storied songwriting team of Betty Comden and Adolph Green. The songs they wrote were designed for Mary's particular voice and character and were a major reason why, as Peter, she made such an indelible impression on her audiences and captured their hearts.

Within her profession, she was not simply admired; she was regarded with reverence and recognized as one of those rare performers who sets the standard of excellence for everyone. Even as a child, I could see the immense respect she had earned: on those occasions when she took me to a Broadway opening night, I would sit next to her at Sardi's, the famed theatrical hangout, sipping my Shirley Temples late into the night and watching as every famous person in the room came over to our table to greet her with so much deference it was as if she were a queen. In a way, she was. She not only loved performing, she truly believed in the power of the performing arts to change lives.

In the years since her death, I have gone to see revivals of her shows like *South Pacific* and *Peter Pan,* and when word would get out that I was Mary's granddaughter, people would come up to me and tell me all kinds of stories about how much her performances had meant to them. I particularly remember the siblings who told me about their parents, who had an interracial marriage and had met while their father served in the South Pacific. They said that because the musical *South Pacific* had dealt so sensitively with the subject of interracial marriage, it had helped their families back home understand that love has no color and that prejudice is taught to us in insidious ways. Women who had been nurses in the Pacific theater during World War II told me they knew just how it felt to want to wash that man right out of their hair. But the show that so many people still hold very dear in their hearts is *Peter Pan.* My grandmother was the embodiment of joy and life in that musical. Older men and women come up to me at the end of a show, eager to tell me how much they loved my grandmother and that they still dream of flying.

Her fans came from all walks of life. One day, as she was crossing Fifth Avenue, a big guy wearing a hard hat emerged from a manhole. Recognizing her instantly, he asked, "Peter, will you crow for me?"

Though she was dressed in her usual, stunning Chanel suit, she planted her legs as far apart as her elegant skirt would allow, placed her hands on her hips and, in the middle of New York's busiest street, let out a loud, guttural, and joyous crow.

One of the most fabled lines in *Peter Pan* came when Grandma, as Peter, asks the audience if they believe in fairies. Peter was her very favorite role from a career that was full of lovable and memorable characters. She truly *was* the spirit of Peter Pan. When anyone she knew was in need of courage, she would get physically close to that person, often crouching down next to him or her in a tomboyish fashion, and then she would quote one of the iconic lines from the show: "Do you believe in fairies?"

Those words, when said by my grandma, were a magical tonic that somehow had the power to infuse whomever she said them to with a new strength.

When she was sixty-nine, that spirit of Peter Pan was still in evidence after she was in a terrible car accident. It was a tragedy that killed two people who were very dear to her—her manager, Ben Washer, who had been living with her for several years and was like a member of the family, and the woman who was like a big sister to her and her closest friend, the film star Janet Gaynor. Though Janet did not die that day, she was so seriously injured in the crash that she struggled in vain for her life for two more years before she passed.

Grandma's injuries were life threatening too: her lung was punctured, two ribs were broken, and her pelvis was broken in three places, yet she remained in the hospital a mere nine days. As she was leaving, moving with the aid of a walker, scores of nurses and doctors gathered and called out after her, "We believe, Mary! We believe!"

The following year, she headlined a benefit for that hospital. At the age of seventy, dressed in her green Peter Pan costume, Grandma "flew" over the audience, crowing and sprinkling fairy dust on the upturned heads of the crowd far below. When she was still wired for sound and was finally set back down on the curtained balcony high above the seated audience, we could all hear her say, from her hidden perch, five words that for me totally exemplify her amazing and ever-youthful spirit. The words were: "Can I do it again?"

At the time I was born, Mary was only forty-five years old and was still playing Peter Pan for a production of the show on TV. She was much too young and spritely to be called "grandmother," so I affectionately called her Ganny. Ganny never forgot her small-town Texas roots, and she wanted to make sure that everyone, not just those who could pay for a trip to New York and a Broadway show, would see her perform. She starred in the touring cast of shows like *Annie Get Your Gun, Peter Pan,* and *Hello, Dolly!,* performing in towns all over the United States and all over the world to bring her gifts to folks where they lived. She truly cared about her audiences, and I think that's part of the reason they cared so much about her. It is really uplifting to hear the many wonderful stories about Ganny from so many who knew her or saw her on the stage. One such story was sent to me by her accompanist and arranger, Louis Magor. It's about a show that Mary was to do with the symphony orchestra in Milwaukee, where the very high price of the orchestra seats had seriously hindered sales.

One morning, Mary received a call from her manager. Because the show was not selling well, their administration asked Mary to cancel.

She told us that she had let the Milwaukee Symphony Orchestra know that she would not cancel. If they wanted to cancel the show, they could, and she would make sure that her friends in the business stayed clear of that orchestra. It was both a defiant move and one that reinforced her image in my mind as the ultimate trouper.

The Milwaukee Symphony Orchestra got busy and did a fairly good job of selling tickets for the show, so by the time we arrived, they had sold all but about 250 tickets, which were for choice center orchestra seats—the most expensive in the theater.

In Milwaukee we stayed at a hotel that was also hosting a convention of the Battered Wives of Wisconsin. The morning of our final rehearsal, as we were waiting in the lobby for our ride to the orchestra hall, a beautiful, well-dressed woman came up to Mary, hugged her, and exclaimed, "Peter Pan!"

She told Mary about her first experience seeing a professional musical.

She explained that she was in Milwaukee as the keynote speaker for the Battered Wives convention, as she was also a former battered wife. Mary asked how many women were at the convention, and she replied, "Two hundred fifty."

I immediately checked to see if those center orchestra seats were still available, and it turned out they were. After a little conference with Mary, it was decided that we would offer them, with the orchestra's compliments, to the women at the convention.

On the spot we gave them to the woman just before she began her speech. The first thing she told the crowd was that she had just run into Peter Pan in the lobby, that "he" had sprinkled fairy dust all over her and them, and that as a result, everyone in the room would be attending the Mary Martin show with the Milwaukee Symphony Orchestra that evening.

After the show, all 250 women came backstage to meet her. She graciously spoke to each of them, signed programs, and gave them a gift of love that sent them home believing in the good people have to offer.

The next day, as we were on our way to the airport, I asked Mary if she had any idea how good she had made those women feel, and she responded, "Do you have any idea how good they made me feel?"

Ganny believed in the transformative power of the theater. She was also amazingly brave. During the height of the Vietnam War, President Lyndon Johnson asked her to perform for the troops. At that time, she was starring in the touring cast of *Hello, Dolly!* This was a grand, big production with lots of sets and actors. When the cast heard that they were being asked to go to the war zone, most of them did not want to go. They did not want to do anything in support of a war that they opposed, a war they did not believe the United States should be involved in. Ganny did not like the war either, but she told them that it was an honor to be asked by the president himself to use their talents as actors to support Americans who were serving our country. These were young people, stationed far from home, who truly deserved to be cheered and entertained. She said that she would go even if no one else did. The cast was persuaded, and after a great deal of planning, Ganny was on her way to Southeast Asia with *Hello, Dolly!*

As soon as she landed at the airport and saw the frightened faces of the people on the ground, my grandma admitted to herself that she did not have a clear idea about the degree of danger into which she was leading her own troops. In Saigon, she could see how difficult and out of control the situation was while being so close to the fighting, but she also saw how eager the soldiers were to have them there.

Ganny was a tiny little person, but she was determined to do all she could to bring the soldiers' spirits up and be a role model for the cast and crew. They could hear bombings very close by as they were setting up the makeshift stage at Nha Trang Air Base. Between shows, she toured the hospitals with General Westmoreland and saw first-hand the devastation of war. The tragedy of the violence she witnessed changed her life; after Vietnam, there was a serious side to her that had never been there before.

A *Life* magazine photographer had accompanied her to Vietnam. He took a great picture for the cover of the magazine; he shot Ganny from behind as she greeted the troops at the end of the show. She had come back onstage as herself, wearing a very feminine, flowing gown, having shed the corseted and plumed Victorian costume of her character. The real Mary was warm and genuine and there to give them everything she could from the depth of her heart. In the pictures, you see her back and, in front of her, the faces of hundreds of soldiers who'd come to see her. What comes across to me as I look at that picture are these hundreds of men (and one or two women) beaming at her, and I knew she had touched their lives with that special gift she had. At the end of one of the final performances, an officer came onstage to read a telegram from President Johnson, a fellow Texan, thanking Mary publicly for her service to her country.

On another occasion, while the Vietnam War raged on, she attended a huge antiwar rally at the New York Public Library. Gathered there were the casts of every single show on Broadway, but when my grandmother, Mary Martin, entered, her fellow performers fell silent and instinctively parted to clear a space for her as she made her way through the crowd. It was a gesture of the utmost respect. There could be no doubt that she deserved the moniker *The New York Times* gave her: "The First Lady of American Musical Theater."

After Dad became the most-watched character on television, he and Ganny often teased one another about who was more famous, a rivalry that went way back and was probably inadvertently fostered by the woman who raised them both, Mary's mother, Juanita. Parenting two generations of children was not without consequences and, in this tricky domestic setup, Mary and Larry had—perhaps inevitably— been rivals for Juanita's love and affection. The flaw in Juanita's caring and parenting was that she had so effectively protected them from each other that they had become less like mother and child than like siblings, and, as such, there was always a degree of competition between them even though they were also mutually supportive. This playful rivalry was illustrated by an incident I witnessed many years later. The two of them were on the street headed to the theater to see Joel Grey perform in San Francisco, and it was hard to get a taxi but when a taxi driver finally did pull up to them he said to my dad, "I'm off duty, but my wife would kill me if I did not pick up J. R." Dad offered the cab to his mother, but the driver said, "No, I want you, J. R."

So Dad got in the cab, and as it pulled away he called out to his mother, saying, "That's showbiz, Mom."

When Joel opened his show, he told the audience that he had two special friends in the audience, Larry Hagman, which was followed by polite applause, and then he said, "And his mother, Peter Pan."

Ganny got a standing ovation that went on for a few minutes, and while smiling all the while, she tilted her head toward Dad and whispered, "And that's showbiz too, baby boy!"

It was around that time that someone said to Ganny that playing J. R. Ewing had made her son an icon. She drew herself up to her full height of five foot two and said, "My son is a star. *I'm* an icon."

When I was in my early twenties, I had a special night with Ganny during which I came to understand how much she missed her mother even decades after Juanita died. Ganny had invited me to stay with her as a guest in her dear friend Dorothy Hammerstein's apartment after we had gone to see Sandy Duncan in *Peter Pan.*

Ganny was delighted to see the show and loved Sandy in her favorite role. And she had been deeply moved when she paid a surprise visit to Sandy's dressing room, and upon seeing her, Sandy had burst into tears. She told my grandma, "You're the only Peter Pan I'll ever know," to which Ganny had graciously replied, "But you see, you are *my* Peter Pan."

My grandma was quite emotional and full of reminiscences that night as she and I tucked under the covers of the big four-poster bed in Dorothy's very elegant apartment. We talked late into the night, and at some point, I began complaining to her about my mother, who I felt was interfering in my life. Usually cuddly, Ganny put a stop to my outpouring when she looked me straight in the eye and said, "Look at you, in your slinky leopard-print nightgown; you look all grown up. Now stop and listen to your whining little girl's voice complaining about your mother. It is time you match your voice with your body and grow up. You can't have it both ways."

Here was my Peter Pan grandma telling me to grow up! Her expression was angry, and because she was so seldom angry with me, I sat up and paid attention. Next, Ganny said, "You will never know what loneliness is until your mother dies."

It was then that I saw a kind of sadness on her face I had never seen before. I had known how deeply my father loved his grandmother, but it was at that moment that I got a sense of what an amazing mother Juanita had been to both of them.

Juanita's death was incredibly hard on my father too. When she became ill and could no longer care for her twelve-year-old grandson, she did not tell him that she was dying from cancer. She said only that she was sending him off to stay with his mother for a while. As he traveled alone on his first solo trip by train from Los Angeles to New York, he did not know that he would never see his beloved grandmother again. But he may have sensed that something was wrong, and I can imagine that this was very frightening to him. Soon after he arrived at the home Richard had created for his mother's new family, he had to face the worst thing that can happen to a child; the one person who had always been there for him was dead. Dad had many mixed feelings about his mother, but he had adored his grandmother without reservation. He must have felt like a lost boy.

Life with his mother certainly did not revolve around a young boy. Ganny was working eight shows a week, and she and Richard had a baby daughter, Heller. In the Martin/Halliday home, children were not the focus; it was each day's performance that formed the center of life.

There was no time for her to grieve with her son; at this point in their lives, they barely knew each other, and though they were both in pain, they didn't speak about their mutual loss.

Whenever Dad spoke about his grandmother Juanita, he got a special tone in his voice; his memories of her were so loving. One of the few times I ever saw tears in his eyes was during a Christmas dinner our family had at Casa del Mar, a grand building in Santa Monica that had just been converted into an elegant seaside hotel. He had just turned eighty years old and, for the first time since he was a child, was back in the same place where his grandmother used to bring him for swimming lessons. As we walked through the lobby to the dining area with the concierge, he asked if the swimming pool was still in the basement. The look on his face told me that he was transported back in the time to the days when his grandmother was caring for him.

5

Real Texas Roots

AFTER HIS BELOVED GRANDMOTHER passed away, the lonely teenaged boy that was my father often behaved in strange and difficult ways. I think this happened because there was no safe place where he could express his sadness, confusion, and sense of abandonment. As he struggled with all these repressed emotions, Richard was downright cruel toward him, and this made Dad's life with his mother and Richard unbearable for him and for them. Richard was a stickler for perfect manners, perfect dress, and perfect adherence to his schedules and plans. All these plans centered on keeping Mary Martin in perfect form for her public, and Dad was barely allowed to see his mom at all. The more Dad acted out, the more it became clear that his stepfather did not like the prospect of living with what he called "a recalcitrant adolescent boy."

So Dad was shipped off to boarding school. Though that sounds harsh, the fact is that his mother was actually trying hard to become the best mother she could be to him. She could see that everyone was uncomfortable with the living situation as it was and the school to which he was sent, the Woodstock Country School in Vermont, was a fantastic place. It was a progressive, coed school that fostered a family-like, egalitarian learning community. She took him there herself, and on the very first day, Dad found Roger Phillips, who became his roommate and one of his very best friends for life. Roger and his loving family have been with us through thick and thin. I have always thought of him as my Jewish uncle in New York, and he is the one I turn to when I miss my dad so much it hurts.

I am sure Dad would have loved to have stayed at Woodstock for his entire high school experience, but after the meticulously supervised life he lived with his grandmother, who had sent him to boys-only military schools, Dad did not handle his newfound freedom well. At Dad's memorial, Roger recounted the incident that—unfairly—got Dad in terminal trouble.

> *Not smoking in the dorms was one of the school's only rules. It was definitely forbidden, but that's what about six of us were doing. We heard someone coming up the stairs and threw our cigarettes out the window. Quickly, smoke filled the air because a fire started when one of the butts lit a dry mop that was on the roof. The dorm master asked, "Who did this?" No one spoke. It was impossible to tell which of the six cigarettes rolling down the tin roof actually hit the mop. After a long silence, Larry said, "I did." And the amazing thing, of which I'm ashamed to this day, is that no one said anything after this. We could have come to his rescue by saying that we all did . . . and we let him take the rap. Larry was suspended.*

Roger never forgot that Dad made it possible for him to stay in school, and his loyal friendship gave my father a stability that was a great comfort to him. As Roger recounted, so many years later, what happened that night in the high school dorm to all Dad's friends and family, tears came to his eyes.

Dad did not last long back in the house with Richard. It was obvious to them all that he was going to have to move again. While he had been at Woodstock, Dad had learned to ride horses, and when his mother and Richard said they did not know what to do with him, Dad said, "Send me to my father in Texas. I want to be a cowboy."

Though he hardly knew his father, he was sure that he would not be like Richard. The stories he heard about his father conjured a picture for the teenaged Larry of a Hemingway-like figure who hunted and fished. So off he went to Texas, where he had not lived since he was a toddler. He was more than ready to go. Texas would be both strange and yet somehow familiar.

My Papa Ben was quite a character who looked very different from my father with his fireplug body and a flattop, but he and my father shared the full, expressive lips that made them both attractive in their own ways. After he and Mary divorced, Ben went to fight in World War II and became a lieutenant colonel, winning a Bronze Star for exceptional and meritorious service on the battlefield. During the war, he married Juanita Saul, who had been his law secretary, and they had a son, Gary. By the time Larry was sent by train to his father, Ben had become a very well-respected lawyer in Weatherford.

From the start, my dad wanted to be just Papa Ben. He felt accepted by his stepmother, who was named Juanita like his beloved grandma. Juanita did not fuss at him about manners like Richard had and Dad developed a real affection for her. Papa Ben lived up to and surpassed any notion my father had of being a manly man. He made up for the years they had been apart and spent a great deal of time with him, and together they did all the "manly" things, like hunting and smoking and drinking. Weatherford was in a dry county, which meant you could not buy alcohol locally, but that did not stop anyone from driving across the county line to fill up their car trunks with bottles of booze; in fact, these pilgrimages added to the ritual of drinking.

As a little girl, I got to know Papa Ben during our many trips to Weatherford. On hot summer nights, I would sit curled up out of the way listening to jokes and stories told under the cigarette haze that swirled around the bare lightbulb while the men played poker and knocked back bourbons on the screened-in back porch. They recounted heroic deeds of the wild things they did while "shitfaced," like when Papa Ben drove a tank through the wall of a German bank toward the end of his service in World War II. He decided it was his right to take bags of cash, and he felt really rich until he learned the currency wasn't worth the paper it was printed on.

After he passed away, one of these drinking stories was the legend of how Papa Ben died. Dad told the story with a big dose of gallows humor, emphasizing his own father's fun-loving spontaneous nature; "Papa Ben had been drinking at a party held at the country club. It was his custom to jump into the pool when he had a few too many, but on this last jump, he was so drunk he didn't notice the pool had no water in it." The abrupt ending to the story lets the listener come to their own conclusions about the consequences of drinking. The real ending to the story was not so sudden, making it even more tragic. Papa Ben lingered in the hospital. He had a series of strokes over the next months, which were probably caused by the injury he sustained when hitting his head on the pool's concrete bottom. He passed away just before the first episode of *I Dream of Jeannie* went on the air. He was only fifty-seven.

After his father died, Dad still spent time in Weatherford, and it was always an occasion for hard drinking. I remember being in the backseat of our station wagon during one of these visits. Dad was driving us back to his stepmother's house in town after dinner at the home of one of his high school friends who lived out in the country. He was so blind drunk that he could not see the road ahead of him. Even drunk Dad was safety conscious so to make sure he would not drive off into a ditch, he cracked the driver's-side door open so he could see the yellow center dividing line up close. Dad took precautions for the fact that he was always drinking; he became a stickler for making sure everyone had their seatbelts securely fastened as soon as the device was invented, but he never stopped driving with a beer in his hand.

He had put us in danger when driving drunk, but he would not have been asking for forgiveness for that. Hell, he probably didn't even remember doing it. It was dumb luck that he was never in a bad car accident, but then, in many ways, he was very lucky.

6

Dad Goes into the Family Business

MARY AND RICHARD WORKED TOGETHER on all her shows, and as part of the team their daughter, Heller, was given small roles in many of them. Dad was in his late teens when he realized he wanted to be in showbiz too. He learned how to get the audience to laugh while doing plays for the Weatherford High School Drama Club, and he was hooked. He tried taking drama at Bard College where his good friend Roger was enrolled, but he dropped out after only one year. Dad told his mother about his newfound love of theater hoping she might find some acting work for him, but the tension that existed between my father and Richard made it impossible for him to be cast in a show with his mother. The fact is, Ganny would really have liked to have had him play a role in one of her shows, but at this juncture in their lives, she knew it would have caused too much family tension. Instead, she helped him get his first few jobs with theater companies like the Margot

Jones Theatre in Dallas and St. John Terrell's theater in Saint Petersburg, Florida.

Dad worked hard and barely earned enough to get by doing these jobs. Living their lavish lifestyle, his mother and Richard could have afforded to help him out with a bit of extra cash, but they were united in their decision not to give him any spending money, because along with his infatuation with the theater, Dad had developed another love; while in high school, he had become a very heavy drinker. This fact was brought home to them when he had stayed with them in Connecticut for a few weeks. While he holed up in his room to stay out of Richard's way, he had gotten very sick. They became very frightened for him when he couldn't get out of bed, so they called in a doctor. After examining him, the doctor told them Dad had drunk so much that he had alcohol poisoning. They did not know how to get him to cut down on his drinking, so their strategy was that they would not give him any spending money, figuring that if he didn't have an extra dime, he wouldn't be able to buy liquor. Instead of drinking less, Dad figured out a way to stop paying rent; he took advantage of the warm nights in Florida and slept outside. He strung up a hammock between the latrines and the dressing rooms and slept there so he could keep partying.

Dad loved telling stories of his early years as an actor. He dramatically claimed he had to steal food to survive. But the truth is he never knew real poverty; he just wasn't any good at holding on to cash. Even after he had started a family and we were living in Malibu, he was always saying he was broke, particularly during the years between *Jeannie* and *Dallas*. Dad worked quite a lot but seemed to spend anything he made as fast as he made it. It was only when he got into his fifties that he finally amassed enough money to stop talking about not having "a pot to piss in."

Dad got together with Mom when he was just twenty-three years old, and from then on, even when his earnings were slight, she always made sure that wherever he lived was beautiful, even the second- and third-rate hotel rooms they stayed in when Dad was in a show on the road. Mom always traveled with candles and nice bed coverings; she would place shells around the room if they were on the coast or put wildflowers in tin cans to brighten a room. After I was born, they would take me along, and she would open a drawer in the bureau of their hotel room, line it with towels and pillows, and transform it into a crib for me. She loved the romance of being on the road with him and didn't really want him out of her sight. I am sure that having us along created a moderating influence on his drinking behavior.

That summer of tough love that Mary and Richard had imposed on my father had lasting effects on him. Dad never forgot about being forced to live on a tight budget, and no matter how much money he made, he never really believed he had any. Even after *Dallas* made him rich and with my mom at his side constantly working to create a cozy home for him, he still felt a deep insecurity. He always liked to have some cash on hand and told me that he liked owning some gold because he didn't trust U.S. currency.

Dad's unusual behavior delighted and amused most people, but sometimes his antics backfired, and folks found him difficult. Predictably, Richard was one of those who never got Dad's sense of humor. Dad loved the attention he got from his antics, and sometimes they were truly outlandish.

For instance, one night in the late 1960s, Mary and Richard were hosting a formal dinner at a mansion they'd rented outside Seattle while on the road with *Hello, Dolly!* It was a typical Richard-style event, which means it was part of his plan to hone Mary Martin's image as the First Lady of the Musical Theater and to further enhance her career. As we pulled into Everett, Washington, on our way back into the States after a camping trip to Canada, we had no idea that Mary and Richard were nearby. We had been on the road for several weeks, and when we pulled into a market to get food, Dad saw on the front page of the newspaper that Mary Martin was appearing at the local theater, starring in *Hello, Dolly!* This was a tour that took her all over the world. Luckily for us, our peripatetic paths had crossed.

Low on cash and in need of a place to bathe, Dad found out where they were staying and drove up to the big, gray, stone mansion, and with rock and roll blaring out of the speakers, we pulled to a stop, and all hopped out of our neon-blue-and-green VW hippie van. Dad was wearing what he called his "Engineer Bill outfit"—striped overalls with a flowered peasant blouse billowing out from under the straps and his ubiquitous rose-pink hippie glasses. The rest of us followed closely behind, tired and dirty; my brother and I hadn't bathed in days. When his startled parents emerged out of the grand entryway, Dad said, "Surprise! What a great place you have here! Can we camp out on the lawn for a few days?"

I could see Richard get really stiff, so uptight that he actually seemed to get taller, and I could tell he was about to lose it when Ganny got her dresser, who traveled with them, to rush us into baths, while the butler hastily rearranged the formal seating for the dinner party they were hosting that evening to accommodate us. Once seated, Dad, who had stopped smoking by this time, pushed Richard even further by blowing soap bubbles in the faces of all the guests who were enjoying their between-course cigarettes, all the while protesting in his booming voice that the smoke interfered with his enjoyment of the food. Cigarette smoking at dinner was the norm then, but there must have been some proper etiquette guidelines forbidding blowing bubbles at the table, because we heard about it the next day and were told that we had to take down the tent from the front yard and be on our way.

By then, Dad so deeply disliked the caustic Richard that he did everything he possibly could to provoke and annoy him. You could argue that he owed Richard an apology for years of this sort of behavior. But I know for certain that it wasn't Richard he was thinking of on his deathbed when he was asking to be forgiven.

7

The Eternal Party

HAVING BEEN SHUTTLED FROM one family to another and never really fitting in, Dad had a particular need to create a family of his own. He kept us close to him always. At the same time, he lived each day as if it were a party, so my mother made it her life's work to create the perfect party environment for him.

The mundane was banished from our existence. In my earliest childhood memories, I have visions of our home life; whenever my parents were not at work, our home was full of people having fun, eating, and drinking; there was the beating of bongo drums and lots of music of every imaginable genre. In the early days, we lived right near Times Square, and Mom transformed an old wreck of an apartment into a bohemian party palace. She was an astute student of all things fashionable. Though she had come from a small town in Sweden, her years in London as a clothing designer had made her a connoisseur of elegance.

She absorbed the lifestyle lessons of my grandma's friends, like socialite Slim Keith, who was one of the greatest hostesses in Manhattan, and was married to Leland Hayward, Ganny's producer. Mom borrowed ideas from these affluent ladies of society about how to light a room and make it smell wonderful; though inspired by this decorous style the apartment we lived in was anything but stuffy and traditional. She didn't need much money to transform it into a place that was truly unique, because Mom knocked out walls and reconfigured spaces in interesting ways. She opened a passageway between the kitchen and dining room and enlarged the door to the dining room to make it an open archway, which led to a big social space she created by tearing down the wall between the bedroom and living room to make one big, open, loftlike space that was the width of the entire front of the building. She covered the wall with fabric and installed a giant bed with built-in lighting and shelves at one end that made it look like a lounging den. When she was given furniture that Ganny's society friends were throwing out, she made slipcovers for them that gave new life to the old, worn Victorian pieces. When they had first moved in, it had been a wreck of a place, but it had lots and lots of rooms, so bit by bit, she transformed the entire floor. Always in need of more money, she rented a room at the back of the apartment to a Swedish masseuse, which added to the exotic Scandinavian allure of our home.

The masseuse liked to practice her craft on everyone; I was getting massages from the time I was a toddler. Another person who lived with us was my aunt BB, my mother's younger sister, who was a nurse and a great cook and had come to help with my birth and just stayed. We were soon joined by another sister from Sweden, my aunt Lillimor, an interior designer. In this household of creative, enterprising women, Dad held court. His friends would drop by with wine and food, and Mom and her sisters would turn whatever they brought into a delicious feast.

My mother, Maj, is Swedish. She grew up in the industrial town of

Eskilstuna, where her father owned a car dealership. The family also owned a farm outside of town that helped them all live decently through the Depression because they grew their own food and grew flax to weave into fabric for new clothes. Mom wanted out of the small-town life and had fantastic energy and ambition. She was a talented artist and was awarded a scholarship to art school, but she had no patience for sitting around in school for a minute longer than she had to. Like Dad, she dropped out of school because she wanted to get on with life. She worked in a clothing factory and gained experience as a seamstress and learned all about manufacturing clothes. She took those skills and became a designer, first in London and then in New York. She and her sisters were strong women who felt that America was a vibrant place that offered more opportunity than they had back home. But they held on to the values that had been instilled in them while growing up in Sweden: respect for self-reliance and nature, the importance of making things with your own hands as a means of controlling your destiny. They were always busy, redecorating the house or analyzing the latest fashions and making their own version of an outfit that was even better than the ones in the magazines. They worked together like a well-oiled machine in the kitchen, and when I was younger, the sisters spoke Swedish together till one day Dad complained that he "did not want to continue to live in a house where he was surrounded by the damn foreigners who speak in a secret language."

As soon as I could, I was standing on a stool to cook with them; we all sewed and painted and cooked together.

One Christmas, Mary and Richard gave my parents a gift of four dozen beautiful, hand-dipped French candles. It was their way of being sensitive to Mom's culture: Swedish people are very fond of using candles to brighten up their dark winters. However, this was at a time when my father was having trouble finding work and was so afraid of not being able to provide for us that he got in the habit of stuffing his pockets with dinner rolls when he went to parties, saying jokingly, "You never know when you're going to be able to get another meal."

The gift of the candles incensed him because it was so extravagant. They were clueless about how broke we were; my dad was too embarrassed to tell them that what we really needed was cash for food.

Dad stormed out into the snow to walk off his frustration, and by some amazing twist of fate, he found a crumpled twenty-dollar bill in a gutter. He came home with bags of food to make a big spaghetti dinner and invited all his friends over. At first, Mom was distraught; she thought Dad had stolen the money. When she heard the whole story, she got into the swing of things. We were going to have a great party! Instead of asking people to bring food, as was the normal custom, she told them to bring flowers. Slim Keith had told her that any dump could be turned into a place of elegance by filling it with candles and flowers. That night, they lit every single candle. The warm glow of so many candles burning at once made winter seem like a distant memory, and their beeswax scent mingled with the many flowers our friends brought, making it feel like a fantastical, dreamy, warm springtime indoors.

If you wanted to have fun, my parents were the people to be with; if you wanted to get serious, Dad usually tuned you out and would start whistling or singing or telling a joke.

But he could also be so warm and patient as he was when I was a toddler and he helped me confront my fear of the dark. Like many small children, I would wake up in the middle of the night afraid of being alone in the pitch blackness. I would run into my parents' bed to snuggle next to them. My exhausted folks tried all sorts of incentives to get me to stay in my own room, like treats and a night-light, but nothing worked. In a final attempt to teach me not to be afraid, Dad took me to the scariest part of our apartment, a fifth-story walk-up on West Forty-Ninth Street, where there was a long, dark, windowless hallway leading to the front door.

I was so scared that every muscle in my body was tight, and I grabbed on to his hand as he knelt down beside me and told me to keep my eyes wide open so that I could let them get used to the dark. He stayed there by my side holding on to me until the dark seemed to take on a benign, velvety quality. After that, I still often came into their bedroom at night, but I wasn't afraid of the dark anymore.

For the first six years of my life, we remained in that apartment, which was right above the Sun Luck Gourmet Chinese restaurant and a triple-X cinema. Occasionally, we ate downstairs at the Chinese restaurant. Pearl, who ran the place, let us eat there on credit. Before moving to America, she had worked in the Chinese circus as an acrobat, and she understood the financial challenges that went with being a performer. She was also a smart businesswoman who ultimately established the most popular Chinese restaurant in the theater district, an elegant place called Pearl's, where stars like Paul Newman could be seen waiting outside, on the street, for a table.

Pearl had kept a thorough accounting of everything we owed her over the years. As soon as Dad got work on a TV series in LA, she asked him to pay up. Dad was disappointed. He always wanted to believe that the pleasure of his company was payment enough.

Sun Luck Gourmet was on the left of the triple-X cinema; on the right, there was a pizza place where ragged-looking children were always hanging around. They wore many layers of clothing, as if everything they owned was on their bodies at once. In Sweden, Mom had been around gypsy kids, and she did not trust these American street children. One day, I said I wanted to wear my long-sleeved shirt under my short-sleeved shirt like the girls downstairs did, but she pointedly told me that I should never try to look like them. One hot summer day, they opened the fire hydrant in front of our apartment and played in the water on the street. I was jealous and wanted to join the fun, but I was not allowed. There seemed to be no rules for fun-loving grown-ups, but there were lots of rules about how I must behave, especially around Richard. With him, I had to be super polite, wear little white gloves, take dainty bites of my food, and only speak when spoken to, and when asked how I was, I should say, "I'm fine, thank you. And you?" while tilting my head and looking directly into the adult's eyes. Those were good manners, and I took direction well, because I knew how important it was to Ganny that I make a good impression on Richard and their guests.

Back in our neighborhood, the streets were full of prostitutes who hung out on corners and in doorways. One day, my mom was struggling to juggle several bags of groceries while keeping hold of my baby brother. She was becoming exasperated because she could not find her keys to open the downstairs door, so she turned to the woman standing nearby and asked her to take the grocery bags for a moment so she could dig around in her purse to find the keys. Hiding behind Mom's skirt, I was fascinated by this woman who had bright-red hair and wore colorful, fancy clothes, but I could see that my mother didn't want me to talk to her. Years later, when I was in my adolescence, my aunts still lived in the apartment, and once, when I was visiting them, I sat at the front window with my friend Bridget Fonda, and we watched as women picked up guys on the street, and, minutes later, we'd see a light go on in the upper floors of the building opposite, and then the light went out and we couldn't see anything anymore. Within an hour, we'd see the same women back on the street.

Dad got a kick out of the fact that our apartment had previously been a brothel run by a famous madam whose customers still showed up from time to time. But because of this, I was never allowed to open the front door unless a grown-up was at my side. I loved running to the door when anyone came because many of my parents' friends didn't have children, and I got a lot of loving attention and candies from them.

When Dad wasn't appearing in a play, he would carry me on his shoulders to West Forty-Fourth Street to see the people arriving at the theater for an opening night. The streets were filled with vibrant nightlife and an amazing variety of signage. On the way there, we could see an enormous billboard at the end of our street, and on it, looming down at us, were the giant faces of Richard Burton and Elizabeth Taylor in an advertisement for the movie *Cleopatra*, both of them looking incredibly glamorous. Just below the billboard was a store that displayed sexy lingerie. Even as a three- and four-year-old I was intrigued by what the dummies in the window were wearing—undies with bright-red lace around cutouts at the nipples and the crotch—but I could not linger for long on why the undies were made like that, because we would quickly approach my favorite billboard on the way to Times Square, a giant coffeepot that was suspended in space above the next building. This was the most amazing advertisement of them all: it had a blinking percolator knob, and it tilted and poured neon coffee into a cup from a spout that had real steam billowing out of it.

Farther down the street, we would walk past the peep shows and topless clubs, where the hawkers outside called out to men passing by as they tried to drum up business. The black curtains just behind them would be cracked tantalizingly open, and music would come blaring out, and Dad would stop in front of it so we could play a game of trying to catch a glimpse of women dancing in the bright lights.

When we got to West Forty-Fourth Street, we'd stand outside the St. James or the Broadhurst Theatre to watch the elegant first-nighters, those beautifully dressed women and men who would emerge from limousines and then wave to the quickly gathering crowd before sweeping into the theater. In those days, an opening night was a black-tie event. The men looked like princes in their perfectly cut tuxedos, and the women in their full-length gowns of satin and lace topped off by jeweled necklaces and tiaras which made them look like princesses in the fairy tales my parents read me at night. It was thrilling to see them. I couldn't wait to grow up and be like them, though of course by the time I was an adult, customs had changed, and opening nights were no longer the all-out glamorous affairs they used to be.

Mom and Dad were often at the theater together. Mom would wait backstage to be with him after the curtain call, and even when Dad wasn't in a show, they wanted to make the scene, watching their friends performing in plays or at a jazz club. It was clear from early on that they needed someone to take care of me. After a few disasters with on-call babysitters, they sought someone who could be hired on a more regular basis. Through the *Irish Times*, they found Peggy, a big, solid Irish widow from "the old country" with teenage girls of her own. As the story has been told to me, when they hired Peggy, Dad was only making around thirty-five dollars a week in the theater. They had to pay her more each week than he was earning as an actor. This made Dad feel that his work was sorely undervalued, and he complained to my mother that they were spending too much on child care. They argued for a few weeks, and in the end, Mom's decision to keep Peggy prevailed.

Mom and Aunt BB were the main breadwinners during this time in our lives, and that gave them authority to allocate how money should be spent. During our early years in New York, these women from Sweden demanded the opportunity to have their own careers and social lives rather than being stuck at home every night with the baby while Dad was out on the town. Dad stopped complaining so much about the money when he saw that having help in the household eased the tension between him and his wife. They began to rely on Peggy more and more, and she always proved worthy of their trust.

In her early adolescence, Peggy had been sent to work on a large estate away from her family, where she would be fed, as they had too many mouths to feed back home. She later told me that her job was polishing the boots of the master of the estate, and though she was not starving, she wanted to get away from that life and come to America to find work. Peggy's life on the estate had instilled in her a clear understanding of workplace hierarchy. Whatever she thought of our bohemian lifestyle, she kept it to herself and always maintained a strong understanding of who was the boss; in fact, that was what she called my father—"the Boss"—and he liked it.

Never saying a word to my parents about how to raise children, she did what she thought was best for me when my parents were out in the evening. She created rituals for me, like learning songs and nursery rhymes, feeding me comfort food, and saying prayers before bed. She insisted on good manners and scolded bad behavior. I always knew where I stood with her. I loved her very much and became very attached to her. She gave me stability in a home where life was very unpredictable.

For example, Peggy would try to convince me to go to sleep before my folks came home, but I always resisted. I knew they were sure to bring a party back home with them, and I wanted to be up so I could join in the fun. Actors get revved up after a show and are not ready to call it a night; everyone was on a tight budget, so Mom and Dad would invite the cast over for a nightcap. Knowing the drill, Peggy sometimes took me to stay at her apartment way up on the East Side, where lots of Irish families had lived for generations. But on most nights, we stayed at our apartment, and when Peggy had successfully gotten me to sleep early, I would still wake up after she was sent home in a cab. As I slept in one of the back bedrooms of our big, rambling apartment, the sounds of music and laughter would drift down the hall; friendly, enticing sounds that would wake me, and I would stir and rub my eyes till I knew where I was, and then I would get up and race down the hall in my nightgown. I was never met with a "hush, hush, get back to bed" attitude from my parents; instead, I was invited to dance on the coffee table to my favorite music, which at the time was the lively staccato rhythms of the composer Khachaturian. I loved being the center of attention. The candlelight flickering on the faces of my parents and their friends as they sat in the living room watching me, I twirled around till I was dizzy and light-headed but nothing would make me stop dancing because I was compelled by the magic of the Slavic music to continue stomping my feet ferociously. This delighted the grown-ups, who would clap and urge me on until at last, completely exhausted, I would tumble into someone's arms and finally curl up in the crook of my dad's arm or make myself a little nest on the pile of overcoats covering the big bed. I would happily drift off to sleep at last with the sounds of music, laughter, the clinking of ice against glass as the drinkers made toasts followed by animated conversation. Those sounds mingled with the scents of perfume and cigarettes filled the air and imbued the soft, warm coats that cradled me.

People often slept over. When I got up in the morning, some of them would still be there, nursing hangovers or eating breakfast or sleeping off the festivities of the night before. One of our most frequent guests was Donny Loomis, a gifted photographer who photographed me from the moment I was brought home, as a newborn, from the hospital. He took many, many pictures: me being held by my proud grandma, who looked glamorous as always, or by my dad as he turned me upside down for fun, absentmindedly holding me as he smoked, or my mom changing me or pushing me in the stroller, or the three of us sleeping together. He also took my father's head shots and documented every-thing we did. He photographed Dad while he was taking singing lessons and during rehearsals. He took trips with us when Dad was in a show on the road, and he documented my first birthday, which we spent in Washington, D.C. While Dad and Donny went to rehearsal, Mom and I were in line to take a tour of the White House. As the story goes, word got out, all the way to President Eisenhower, that Mary Martin's granddaughter was in the building. He insisted that we be brought into his office. My mother was very nervous and also tongue-tied; she couldn't say a word. She later told me that the president was very kind to us and asked why we had come for a visit. Mom blurted out that we were in the White House to celebrate my first birthday, and he said he was amazed to see us because he did not believe that Peter Pan could be a grandma!

Sadly, that was one of the very rare occasions that Donny missed. He seemed to be with us night and day and the photographs he con-stantly took recorded many aspects of my early childhood. These photos were not random snapshots, they were all shot with his profes-sional eye. Though he did take some obviously posed pictures of our family, the most interesting of these images are of us doing the most basic things, like walking down the street and playing at the zoo. He took one of me standing on the toilet seat cover while watching my father brush his teeth; in one of the photos taken that morning, my dad leans over to kiss me with his foamy mouth and his toothbrush still in one hand.

Donny also took some great photos of us on our roof. That roof was an urban kid's version of a backyard. It was where Mom set up a blow-up splash pool for me. Donny took lots of pictures of me playing in the pool, skipping nude in the sprinklers and spraying my mom with the hose. Donny was there with his camera during late-night picnics on the roof when everyone would be wrapped up in beaver coats and blankets and Mom would set up candles and a hibachi grill. Dad played the guitar, and his friends would sing while looking up at the stars from our tar beach right in the middle of midtown Manhattan.

Donny frequently photographed me when we were the only ones up in the morning; one time, when I was three years old, he found me walking around drunk. He was scared for me and woke my aunt BB, who was a nurse. He told her that I had finished off the dregs of wine our guests had left in their glasses the night before, so the two of them walked me around until I was sober. It became one of the standard household jokes that, in the Hagman home, even little kids got drunk.

One of Donny's photoshoots is full of photos of me lying nude on the end of my parents' empty bed, staring inquiringly at the photographer. One of them was framed and hung in our house for most of my life. In the other photos from that session, I am twisting and turning, flirting with the man behind the camera. We have stacks of contact sheets of other photos Donny took, strips of tiny fading images, each revealing our lives unfolding as fast as Donny could click the shutter of his camera, but for some reason the only pictures we have any negatives for are the pictures of me, naked and flirting with Donny. Over the years since my early childhood, I have looked at the huge box of photos Donny left us so many times. They have kept my very early memories alive.

Stories of child abuse are so omnipresent in our culture these days that there have been times when I felt uncomfortable about the nude photos of me, but Donny died when I was four years old, so I will never really know what he intended or why we only have these negatives and not all the others. Donny was a kind and gentle man, and I cannot imagine that he ever meant to use these photos for anything unseemly, nor do I remember anything inappropriate or malicious in his attitude or his behavior toward me. I prefer to think that these pictures are his gift to me, the enduring, tangible memory of my baby self, and they were tools that helped me remember my early childhood.

I recall so many other things that were not photographed too. For instance, the pictures on the roof reminded me that it was where my folks took my German shepherd puppy, named Fraja, to relieve herself when they didn't want to venture out to walk her late at night. Dad would race her up the stairs so she would not pee in the house. Dad often had a quick temper in those days, and he took it out on my dog. He was a real disciplinarian with her. If she barked or chewed something up, as puppies will do sometimes, he hit her aggressively, and as he hit her, he looked at me intensely, saying, "You have to catch dogs in the act and punish them right away, or they will never learn." His gaze was frightening, and I would come to know it later in life when I did anything he disapproved of. Many years later, the whole world would know that same gaze, because Dad, in the role of J. R. on the TV show *Dallas*, looked straight into the camera in just the same way he had looked at me when he was letting me know that he had to hurt my dog for her own good. When he got that look on his face, the TV audience knew J. R. meant business and that he was about to destroy one of his rivals.

It scared me to watch him discipline my beloved dog. His behavior toward Fraja made her a bit touchy. She was very protective of me and sensitive to my moods. She followed me everywhere. I think German shepherds tend to get especially attached to one person, because when I was four and my brother was born, she growled at the new baby. My father immediately sent my dog away, which broke my heart and didn't make me particularly happy about this new addition to our family.

Before Preston was born, my folks did everything they could to convince me to stay in my own bedroom at night so they could be alone. Very often, even after I had ceased to fear the dark, I would have bad dreams and wake up in the middle of the night and tiptoe into my parents' room, which was on the other side of our large L-shaped apartment. To get there, I'd pass the kitchen, dining room, and the bedroom suite with its own sitting room, where Aunt BB lived. I'd race past that scary hallway that led to our front door, and at last, I would get to the biggest room in the apartment, where Mom and Dad slept. The room filled the whole width of the building and had tall leaded-glass windows. People might be sacked out at one end of the room on the couch, but I knew I'd find Mom and Dad in the king-sized bed with the elegant bedding Mom had sewn for it. I would creep in next to them, and they would adjust to my presence without waking.

Once there within the sound of their breathing, I would feel safe, surrounded with love and the scents of their familiar bodies. In this blissful state, I would fall asleep watching the brightly colored neon lights from the restaurant and cinema on the street below as they flashed on and off, like glowing rainbows, across their bedroom ceiling.

8

Set Free in the Wide-Open Country

D AD LIKED TO BE on the move and, in his determination to give us the family closeness he never had, he brought us all with him wherever he went, be it for work or pleasure. We often drove from New York to LA so Dad could work on both coasts; to make it more fun, they found different routes, often stopping in my dad's home of Weatherford, Texas. These were wonderful times during which we would hunt and fish and swim nude in clear mountain streams. Even outdoors, Mom made sure we had a cozy place to rest for the night. She prepared great food on the camp stove while Dad got a big, roaring fire going. Once the fire was big enough, the bugs wouldn't bother us, and we ate around the campfire beneath the sparkling dome of stars. After dinner, Dad would tell wonderful stories or play his guitar and sing to us.

Camping was cheap, which made it a perfect pastime when Dad was out of work. Out in the wilderness, my dad was really relaxed. Even when he wasn't working, Dad was always on, entertaining everyone around him; I think actors who have a calling to the craft are naturally this way. But on camping trips, we were our own tribe, there was no one to impress and no need to dress or behave in any certain way. Dad believed that being in nature was good for the soul. During his teenage years, his happiest times were on horseback in the Vermont countryside and out hunting with his papa. He shared his love of the outdoors with us and taught us to respect nature.

My parents longed for as much time outdoors as they could get. Some New Yorkers are happy living indoors all the time, but one of the things that kept Mom and Dad together was their love of nature. So we got out of the city as often as possible.

Sometimes we stayed with David Wayne, an older actor who had had a huge success as the leprechaun in the hit musical *Finian's Rainbow*. Dad and David had worked together and became good friends; we were always welcome at David's beautiful, big home in Connecticut. But when my ingenious proto-hippie folks wanted to really let loose, they found all sorts of ways to stay out in the country for free. One of the best of these destinations was Sterling Forest, just an hour from the George Washington Bridge. Through Ganny, Mom and Dad made friends with John Houser, who was a Hilton Hotel executive.

The Housers let our family use a little run-down cabin from the time I was a baby until I was seven and we moved away from the East Coast. The cabin was across the road from a waterfall, just a ten-minute walk from the Housers' grand Japanese-style home that overlooked a lake. John was a bit older than Dad, but the two men became best friends who swam in the lake at all hours and drank and sang and played cards together. The cabin he lent us was a wreck; the paint was peeling, and there was no glass in some of the windows, but the fresh scents and the sounds of birds and the brook flowing by were so welcome after the noise and gritty air of the city that no one cared about how the place looked. We could never seem to get enough of it. In Sterling Forest, I was free to roam around all day, accompanied only by my dog.

For another change of scenery, we would go camping in the sand dunes of the Hamptons, out on the end of Long Island, a few hours from New York City. This was a very beautiful beach community where the real estate was wildly expensive even in those days, but camping was nearly free. To get there, we would go with a group of friends in a caravan of cars driving though potato fields and lush farm country, where my folks would stop to buy enough fresh corn and tomatoes to last the long weekend. On one of these trips, they saw an abandoned refrigerator on the side of the road and somehow got it towed to our regular camping spot. They dug a really deep hole and put the fridge in it; that way the fruits and vegetables stayed fresh in a giant insulated cooler. When they left they covered it over with sand and put some rocks and driftwood across it so that they could dig it up the next time we were there.

At the campsite, Dad and all his buddies, like Jimmy Hammerstein (Oscar's son), wore sarongs, a wrapped skirt-like piece of clothing that Dad's friend John Houser had introduced him to. Houser had learned how to live the good life while working for Hilton in Southeast Asia and the Pacific Islands; he called this form of skirt a "Lava-lava." Away from the city and 1950s dress codes, the men dispensed with pants. Dad always loved to show off his shapely legs. He never like to wear pants when he did not have to. The guys would dive in the ocean wearing these loose flowing wraps. All things Hawaiian were popular then, and they also used what was called a Hawaiian sling—a harpoon with a giant rubber band on the end—to catch fish for our dinner. The guys got a great kick out of going native, walking around the dunes dressed like Pacific Islanders in an ocean paradise just hours from the big city.

We did not always stay close to New York. We took many cross-country trips, during which we saw much of the United States. As I grew older, though I still could not help with the driving, I did learn how to read maps and enjoyed being the copilot, helping Mom or Dad navigate the countryside. Back then, you could camp almost anywhere, and in the late afternoon, we would leave the main highways and travel narrow country roads. When we saw a promising dirt road, we would follow it until we came to open land. In order to make sure we were not camping in someone's driveway, we would search around a bit, and if the coast was clear, we would park and set up our tents.

The first thing Dad would do when we got to a campsite was clean it up. Environmental consciousness had not yet become popular with the general public, and many of the off-road places we camped in were covered in garbage. Dad took us kids all around the area where we were going to stay, picking up debris and collecting wood for our campfire. This was our way of making the place our home; it gave me and my brother a chore to do and a chance to stretch our legs. Dad made you feel like you were contributing to our family's happiness and well-being, praising us for collecting as much wood as we could carry and telling us which type of wood burned the longest and which was good for kindling to start the fire with. While we were busy doing this, Mom set up camp. She had designed and sewed a canopy out of mosquito netting, rip-stop nylon that had zippered doorways. The whole contraption was hung on poles attached to the roof of our Jeep. This created a bug-free room connected to where all our stuff was stored in the car; it also marked the area that served as our kitchen. Before the fire was started, she would have pulled out the camp stove and cutting board, and as we foraged for wood, we knew where our camp was by the delicious scents of her cooking, which drew us back from the surrounding forest.

We often stayed on the shores of lakes or streams, and since we always tried to camp far from any other people, we did not bother with bathing suits; we just took our clothes off and dove right in. Or if we were in one place for a while, we never bothered putting anything on until evening when it became cool. Camping in the wilderness with no one around for miles, we played in and out of the water all day long. It was perfectly natural for our family to be naked. As a child, I was always comfortable with my clothes off. Maybe this was a Scandinavian thing. Being next to water meant we always had something to do, swimming or fishing or just playing in the water's flow. As sunset approached, we would get quiet and keep a lookout for the animals that would come to drink at the water's edge. But water can be dangerous too: one time in the middle of the night, we discovered we were on a tidal flat as water rushed into our tent, covering us in our suddenly sodden sleeping bags.

As we passed through different temperate zones, my folks made sure we learned about the plants and animals native to the places we stayed in. In Canada, we saw moose; in the Southwest, we were introduced to coyotes and jackrabbits. We learned how to spot holes that might have snakes in them and knew which types of trees were the lookout posts for birds of prey. Dad taught us which birds were good for eating and how to hunt for them. He never hunted big game like deer or bear, but we had more than one run-in with bears, who love to steal food from campers, and we knew never to keep our food in the tent with us. Nowadays, there is a whole industry around camping and outdoor adventure, but the way we went camping looked very different and far more basic than all the advertisements you see for fancy camping equipment. We did not hike or climb mountains; we would just establish a camp and live there hunting, fishing, or just hanging out for a few days in nature.

In the course of long, leisurely days, the folks would read and drink wine. My brother and I would make forts and dam up sections of a river, moving rocks and pieces of wood around to make its course change. We looked at beaver dams and tried to make ours just as big and strong. These projects would keep us busy all day. Mom was the best angler among us; she was very patient and very lucky. She would cook the fresh fish on an open fire. Everything tastes better when you have been outdoors and the air is clean and you have been playing hard, moving around all day just for the fun of it.

One memorable spot we stayed in was an abandoned logging camp near the Canadian border. We were there for a few days on the edge of a glacier stream. I have a picture of us naked with the ice-cold water dripping off of us as we pose for Mom's camera. When we were not hunting or looking for animals, our campsite was filled with music. We would bring along a portable record player and blast the music really loudly with no neighbors to hear us. Dad and I sang along with Barbra Streisand at the top of our lungs as her rendition of "Cry Me a River" echoed off the canyon walls in the beautiful, lonely hinterland. We brought jazzy urban music to the wilderness, and the clash of realities made each sweeter. It was as if we had the entire country to ourselves. We always left each campsite as pristine as possible when we finally drove off.

Mom and Dad had a book called *The U.S. Interior Guide to Thermal Springs.* That book helped us plan our camping trips so that every few days we would hit one of the hot springs to bathe in. Some were just holes in the ground filled with other naked hippies like ourselves. But others were in beautiful bathhouses, like the ones in Hot Springs, Arkansas, that were modeled on the great spa towns of Europe. These bathhouses were remnants of a time before antibiotics, when these health-promoting waters provided sick people with one of the few hopes for getting well. Back in the day, if you were ill, you might spend weeks at the bathhouse in Georgia or Arkansas, but by the early 1960s, modern medicine had left these institutions practically empty; they were abandoned Victorian palaces. The few attendees left in these resorts that had gone out of fashion were as ancient as the buildings themselves, and they were overjoyed to meet a whole young family of bathing enthusiasts.

When we actually took "the baths," the attendants separated the men and the women. After you took your clothes off, they wrapped you in big white sheets and moved you from one bath to another of varying temperatures. At one point, they closed you into a metal box with a hole for your head to poke out of: it looked like a torture chamber from some strange dystopian movie, but it was in reality an early steam bath. Toward the end of the "cure," they wrapped you up tight in yet more sheets till you were like a giant swaddled baby, at which point you were left to lie down and rest in a darkened room so you could have time to savor the health-giving effects of the water treatment.

I have made pilgrimages to Hot Springs, Arkansas, several times on my own over the course of the many years since we first found it in near ruin. The place is now quite a tourist town. Some enterprising residents have capitalized on the feeling that when you go there, it feels like you are living in a bygone era. It is at the edge of a huge national forest, and for me, going back there is a journey to one of the many adventures of my childhood.

Later, when Dad was working in television and we had settled in LA, my folks found places we could go to regularly to get out of town. We went to an Italian place in Ojai where there was a huge, beautiful field to picnic in; we went to Solvang, which is a Danish-style village near the vineyards of the Santa Ynez Valley and where the folks could do some wine tasting. When the schedule was tight, we'd head for the big sand hill just north of Malibu, and we'd slide down it, toward the ocean. And if we really were pressed for time, we'd head off to the Santa Monica Pier that stretched out over the Pacific Ocean and where we'd have dinner and take a ride on the vintage merry-go-round and play in the arcade.

But one of the best places we visited regularly was a rustic getaway called the Double Rainbow Ranch; it belonged to Barton MacLane, Dad's fellow actor and dear friend on *I Dream of Jeannie*. On the show, Barton's character, General Peterson, was often angry at Dad's character, Tony Nelson. That was funny to me because their offscreen relationship was very warm, almost paternal. Barton was something of a cowboy. On his ranch, he was Western through and through. At night, Barton's friends would come around to the back porch to sing folk songs. One would bring a washtub bass, another would bring a ukulele, and Dad would play guitar. Barton was as rugged a man as anyone could ever find, but he sang love songs with this sweet, super-high-pitched falsetto voice that amazed me as a young girl. I loved sitting with them, looking up at the sky filled with so many stars. They showed me which ones were not stars but satellites, and I learned all about Sputnik, which was launched just before I was born. Barton took Dad hunting, and he became something of a father figure to him. Their relationship came at a perfect time because my dad's own father, Papa Ben, had died just before the first episode of *Jeannie* aired. I am sure that hunting on Barton's ranch made Dad feel close to his departed father, and this was where I remember learning to shoot a gun. We shot rabbits because, as Barton told us, rabbits were a nuisance to ranchers; they ate everything and kept multiplying. Barton and his neighbors paid a dollar apiece for each rabbit any of us killed, and back then, I hunted too. We shot so many rabbits that we had to dig a big pit to bury all the pelts and guts in. We sat at the edge of this pit, skinning the animals and throwing the bloody fur into it so that Dad could cover it over before nightfall and keep the coyotes and other scavengers from coming around.

My aunt BB also got excited about shooting bullfrogs. Frogs legs were a French delicacy, and she had learned how to cook them when she apprenticed to the head cook at a castle in Sweden before she became a nurse. She was an excellent cook and thought, for a time, that she might become a chef.

BB was a good shot, and one day, she killed a bunch of frogs. But because frogs are cold-blooded, they don't die easily; the legs still hopped around even after they were cut from the bodies, and it was quite a sight seeing them hop around the skillet as BB poured wine on them as they cooked. A few years later, I started to get squeamish about killing things. It no longer seemed like fun to me, and Dad naturally excluded me from his hunting life.

Dad also took my brother and me on location with him when he went overseas, even when it meant pulling us out of school, because he believed we could learn more by seeing the world and being with him than by sitting behind desks being fed the same information everyone else was getting. At first when we were in grade school, it didn't make much difference to our education, like when I was six and my brother just two and we went to Rome for several months. Dad was doing a film called *The Cavern,* and Mom did not have to work. She rented a tiny Fiat 500 and took us to all the museums and street markets and to the Sistine Chapel again and again. At times, we were the only people in the big, high-ceilinged hall, and she would have us lie on our backs so we could look up at the splendor Michelangelo had created. The Coliseum was full of wild cats we would feed regularly, and I fell in love with octopus pasta on the Amalfi Coast.

On another occasion, Dad was making a movie in Chile with Trini Lopez, who was known mostly as a singer. For part of the time, we stayed at an abandoned whaling village far from any civilization. We took long walks in the countryside at night, and Dad taught us about the different stars you could see in the Southern Hemisphere. I was studying Spanish; no one else in my family spoke any Spanish, and I translated as best as I could when we needed to buy train tickets and such. In an attempt to improve my language skills, I read the newspapers, and I learned quite a bit about the political struggles going on in Chile while we were there. It was a very volatile and dangerous time due to the fact that the Chilean people had elected Salvador Allende, the first Marxist to become president of a Latin American country. This was in 1973, and when I went back to school, I had a lot to talk about with my Spanish teacher. Soon after we returned home, President Allende was assassinated.

These trips formed who I am today. My parents provided us with an eccentric, rich education. And Dad was proud of having raised us so differently from other kids. He was never apologetic about that. Certainly, our unusual upbringing was not what was haunting him at the end of his life, when he kept saying, "Forgive me."

9

Life Above the XXX Cinema

A S A CHILD, I delighted in going to the theater, especially when it was to see Dad or Ganny in a show.

I was three years old when Ganny gave me a theater trunk with a big gold star painted on it that was filled with costumes, which included tiny Victorian high-necked gowns, cowgirl dresses, and a Chinese jacket and pants made of embroidered silk. Whenever I went to the theater to see her or Dad, they would be in costume, so I would visit them completely outfitted in one of my very own costumes.

Ganny was starring in *The Sound of Music* then, and Dad had a good role in a play called *The Beauty Part*. I was such a regular backstage at both of their shows that the stagehands would set up a tall stool and make a little cigarette hole in the backdrop so I could peek through it and watch the show from center stage and see the audience.

I loved my little perch and sat there as quiet as a mouse, but I am sure there are all sorts of safety rules that would make it impossible for a kid to do that these days. I watched *The Sound of Music* so many times that I thought I knew all the words and cues and songs; I secretly wished the youngest girl in the Von Trapp family would get sick one day and I would be asked to take her place.

I became awestruck at this early age by the power of live performances in a theater. One night, when Mom and I came to visit after a show, I let go of my father's hand while the grown-ups were talking and carefully stepped onto the stage. I was a very small person alone on the dark proscenium jutting out into the theater with nothing but the single bulb of the ghost light on; the place was silent, but my ears were still ringing, and all my senses were so alive that I could feel the vacuum left by the recently departed crowd. It was an amazing feeling to be where the actors had been performing less than an hour before. I felt all tingly, transported by the awareness that the physical space I was standing on held an energy that lingered there, left by the magic that the actors had so recently created. I was standing on the exact same spot where those actors had commanded the attention of the entire audience. That audience was filled with individuals who walked in the doors of the theater carrying with them all the joys and sadness of their everyday lives, and once the lights went down, they gave themselves over to the actors, who in turn took the attention they were given and turned the occasion into a communal experience during which people came together to share intense emotions. The theater was a sacred place. It was larger than life, and for years it was the centrifuge of everything our family lived for.

When I was seven or eight, Ganny painted a picture of me standing in front of the cheval mirror that was in her gigantic penthouse bedroom. She loved to paint but rarely painted faces or hands because they required too much detailed work, but this painting was an exception.

She painted my happy, smiling face exactly as it appeared when reflected in her mirror. She stood behind me as she painted, so the picture showed both my mirrored image and my back. I stood very straight; perfect posture was important to Ganny. My long blond hair cascaded down and was held in place by a bow that was the exact same color as my pink velvet dress. I distinctly remember how that dress felt on my body, how it fit me tightly under the arms and swung out into the crisp A-line shape that was fashionable at the time. I was precociously aware of how clothes fit because my mother was a clothing designer, and I liked wearing Ganny's hats, because unlike her dresses, her hats fit me perfectly. Ganny let me have free rein to play with everything in her closet and dressing room. Next to the walk-in closet that smelled like Ganny, she had an antique chest of petite drawers, each just the right size for one cap or dainty hat. These hats were works of art with veils and flowers or feathers. They had no utilitarian purpose; they were hats with attitude and created strictly for beauty and pleasure. I would carry armloads of them across the room to the big mirror so I could check out how great they looked. I felt very grown up wearing them, and I would try them on for hours with Ganny suggesting how a hat should be tilted or adding a scarf to my ensemble. When she was satisfied with my appearance, she would step back and say, "Egads, you look simply *marvelous*, my dear." Neither of us ever tired of the game, and a game it was: I was never allowed to wear the hats outside on the street. They were treats just for the privacy of her big room, where she was my best playmate.

Getting dressed to go out in public was something else. There were lots of rules about how a little girl should look when we went out together. I could only wear my hair pulled back with a matching headband or the right size bow, nothing too big or showy. Then there were all the necessary accessories that every properly dressed little girl had to wear. No one today could imagine the fuss that was made about what must be worn to go shopping at the department store. The requisite outfit included the previously mentioned little white gloves as well as ankle socks neatly folded above my shiny, polished patent leather Mary Janes. These shoes were flats, of course, as any shoe with even the tiniest heel was *tacky,* so Ganny said, on a girl my age. I was often reminded about how I must behave, down to the folding of my hands so I would not twiddle my hair and the crossing of ankles so my feet would not swing as they hung down from my chair. I was made to understand that my behavior was being watched, that everyone's eyes were looking at us when I was out with Ganny because Ganny was a star.

She began taking me on special shopping trips just before Easter when I was just four years old. The approach of spring after the long, cold winter was a magical time in New York. Our neighborhood was particularly gray and dirty in the winter. Unlike Ganny's neighborhood where there were planters full of pine trees and awnings and jolly doormen with uniforms that had big brass buttons on them, on our street there were girly posters pasted up and cheap restaurants and liquor stores so Peggy kept me indoors to play. But she still found lovely places to take me while my mother was working. She was a Catholic, and she walked me to Saint Pat's, which was close by, and once inside the church, we could smell the incense and see the candles lit below the pictures of saints and angels with beautiful wings. As spring approached, she and I spent more time walking in the park where the forsythia would sprout its yellow blooms and the primroses and daffodils began poking through the remaining snow and tree after tree seemed to ready itself to burst into glorious yellow or pink blossoms.

In my home, there was a lot of preparation and excitement leading up to Easter, not the least of which was buying the perfect Easter outfit to wear in the Easter parade. A few days before the big event, Ganny would pick me up in her chauffeur-driven Rolls-Royce Silver Cloud, which would pull up to our apartment building right in front of the triple-X cinema. One of my parents would walk me down the five flights of stairs to the grimy street below. The chauffeur would open the backseat door, and I would hop into the car and enter a different world. Inside, Ganny would be dressed in a chic designer suit with one of her precious little pillbox hats placed jauntily on her head. Around her neck, she wore several layers of pearls interspersed with diamonds, and her shapely legs would be crossed in such a way as if to demonstrate to me how it should be done. As she sat on the creamy leather upholstery of the big backseat, she would be sipping a cocktail. My drink, a Coca-Cola on ice, would be ready for me in a glass on the mahogany minibar in front of my seat.

Then, the Rolls would head a few blocks east and then north to Bonwit Teller or Saks Fifth Avenue. These were enormous stores, with ceilings that extended several stories high and glass counters everywhere on which would be displayed a profusion of perfumes or lipsticks or pastel-colored scarves and hats. In those days, women dressed up to go shopping, and there were ladies everywhere, most of them trying to look like Jackie Kennedy, which meant they were all immaculate in their straight skirts, matching jackets, and what had become the required pillbox hat. There were also beautiful women walking around dressed in evening gowns. These were the store's models, who styled themselves as much as possible to look like Grace Kelly. It was a mind-boggling sight to someone my age; these stores were another world.

We would take the elevator upstairs, and when we arrived at the girls' department, we'd be rushed past all the brightly colored, beautifully frothy dresses. The plan was that we would be sequestered away from all the other shoppers, hidden in the privacy of our extra-large, mirrored VIP dressing room that had several elegant chairs in it. Once we had caught our breaths, we were greeted by our own private shopper. The shopper would of course be very elegantly dressed, and I had been instructed to curtsy to her, and this would prompt her to exclaim how cute I was, and then very discreetly, she would tell my grandma that she was a huge fan of hers and she had seen *The Sound of Music* several times and that it would be such an honor to help us find the right outfit for me. She would listen intently to Ganny's very specific instructions about the perfect au courant ensemble she envisioned for me. The shopper then went around the children's department selecting outfits and hats that my fashion-conscious grandmother would delight in and Richard would approve of. I always wanted frilly, gaudy dresses with lots of lace, ribbons, and bows, preferably in some shade of pink or purple, and I know I made a bit of a fuss about it, but I never even got to try on the gaudy things that attracted me. Instead, we always left the store with me dressed in something elegant and restrained that had no lace, few bows, and absolutely no purple.

One outfit I remember vividly was an empire-style dress that was white with a delicate French toile pattern in black and a small black velvet bow, coupled with a black coat that had three-quarter-length sleeves and came with a broad black velvet headband. The next year, probably because I had voiced more than one complaint about being forced to wear black and white, my beloved Ganny bought me a more modern bright-green A-line dress with a big yellow flower on it.

All decked out in my new finery, ready for the parade the next day, we were dropped off at the 21 Club for lunch. The club had been a speakeasy during Prohibition. When I got older, I was told how the bar could tilt on a fulcrum if the feds raided the place so all the glasses and booze could slide through a trapdoor into the basement on a moment's notice. The bartenders would then place tea and coffee cups where the drinks had been.

The 21 Club had been founded around 1930, but forty-five years later, it still felt like you had to be someone special to get into the place. It was never a "members-only" club, but they fussed over you as if you were a "member," especially if you were famous or happened to be a friend of the Kriendler and Berns families, who were the owners.

To enter 21, you walked through iron gates and past ornamental iron jockeys whose attire was painted in the bright primary colors of the best-known racing stables. The ceiling in the bar–dining room seemed low because there was an amazing assortment of sporting and corporate memorabilia hanging there, everything from toy planes and trains to football helmets to stuffed animals that had belonged to patrons or represented their companies. This increased the feeling that 21 was a clubhouse. The maître d' presented all the ladies with red carnations. Special little girls like me were given gifts like a little silver pin in the shape of a bow with a tiny replica of the signature gates of 21.

Celebrity patrons had their own favorite tables. We were always seated at a big, round table in the front corner, where we could see and be seen by all who came in. Easter was one of our favorite times for lunch at 21. Everyone entering the room would come over to greet Ganny and comment on our Easter outfits. One year, I was invited by the cook to come dye Easter eggs in the 21 kitchen, a special treat.

I always knew the 21 Club was one of the best restaurants in New York, but while the service from waiters in white jackets was impeccable and there was fancy food like steak and oysters, they also featured plain, down-home cooking. Granny's favorite was their famous chicken hash.

She knew without asking what I wanted. She would look at me with her chin tilted and say, "Heidi will have a burger and french fries!"

After lunch, Dad liked to see each outfit Ganny had bought me with all their accessories. He would insist that I parade up and down in front of him and twirl around, as if I were a model on a runway. Mom and Dad always liked the experience of buying clothes, and they loved getting dressed up for special occasions. When Dad died, there was evidence of their love for shopping in several giant walk-in closets full of their clothes, many of which they hadn't worn in decades and others with the tags still on them.

On Easter weekend, some member of my family always took me to see the Rockettes' holiday show, just up the street at Rockefeller Center. And then came the best part: walking hand in hand with Dad in the Easter parade on Fifth Avenue going right past good old Saint Patrick's Cathedral where we would poke our heads in to hear the music. Dad and I loved looking at all the women wearing fantastic pastel-colored hats and matching outfits; the men dressed up too, whole families walked together, and everyone was dressed to the nines. Dad really enjoyed parades; he loved the hubbub and colors and crowds and the sounds. A parade was one of his favorite places in the world to be, and later in Malibu, he became known for creating parades that had no other purpose than to celebrate life.

Only much later did I realize that my pre-Easter shopping excursion with Ganny was her way of readying me to be seen with Dad when he would have his time in the limelight. During the *Dallas* years, photographers often came around when we were on our way out for a meal or after the theater, trying to catch a photo of us and when she saw them, Ganny would tilt her head to highlight her best features and as she did so she would whisper in my ear, "Find the light, so you can look your best."

Both my dad and Ganny knew how to find that light, just as they knew how to grab the attention of people when they were out in public. From holding court at the 21 Club to Dad's hippie parades on Malibu Beach, they set the tableau, created the scene; they wrote the script. For them, the lines between life and the theater were always blurred. The week leading up to Easter was an especially memorable show they created, and I was an important supporting actor for my proud, loving father strolling down Fifth Avenue in the Easter Parade, showing off his little daughter.

The shopping trip with Ganny was also a vivid illustration of the strange dual reality I would live in for most of my life, straddling two sides of a cultural divide simultaneously. After our luxurious day excursions, I would be chauffeured home and dropped off at a building where prostitutes were soliciting in the doorway, and Ganny would go back to her apartment building where the doorman rushed to help her out of her car.

This disparity in living standards and lifestyles was played out again when I moved away to go to college. Dad had never thought to put any money aside for higher education, so when it was time for me to go to university, he told me there was not much money to spare. The truth was that neither of my parents really understood how much money they had and they did not plan for things like education or retirement, especially before they had a consistent income with the success of *Dallas*. Once we moved to LA, they always had a business manager of some kind, someone who paid the bills and took care of the finances. But for several years, these money managers changed often, and there was not much continuity to any financial plan; consequently, if things went bad, there was someone to fire and blame for bad management, but it also meant that neither of my parents understood the big picture about what things really cost.

When it came time for me to apply for college, I was completely on my own. There was no discussion of where or how or if I should go to college. The teachers at my private high school assumed everyone would go to college, and so I began to look into how to do this myself. I had a learning disability, school had been difficult for me, but I had worked with a dance therapist who had helped me overcome the self-esteem issues I had around being dyslexic, and I had begun to really enjoy school. I was inspired to pursue a degree in this branch of therapy. It was a relatively new discipline, having just been recognized ten years earlier, in 1966, with the founding of the American Dance Therapy Association. The organization's Web site describes this therapy in the following way:

> *The psychotherapeutic use of movement is a process which furthers the emotional, social, cognitive, and physical integration of the individual . . . Children who don't have the patience or attention span for other forms of therapy can benefit from the openness that comes with expressive dance. Adults whose emotions have been buried or who are not in touch with their feelings, as well as victims of abuse who are otherwise unable to articulate their problem, may find insight and release through dance.*

Doing dance therapy and feeling better about myself gave me a new confidence that resulted in my ability to get better grades as my concentration on academics improved. I wanted to help others as I had been helped. Mom and Dad did not understand it and did nothing to help me navigate this path toward my adult life—nor did they stand in my way. This field of therapy was so new that I could not find a college that offered a dance therapy degree. The therapist I had been seeing in Malibu suggested I meet with Allegra Fuller Snyder, who was the head of dance and dance ethnology at the University of California, Los Angeles. She wrote a course of study for me and suggested that I apply to Lone Mountain College in San Francisco. They accepted me and agreed to follow the plan that had been written for me. I was so enthused about beginning my studies that I headed straight to college that first summer after high school instead of joining my family on location in Ireland, where Dad was making a film. Getting into a college and having a course of study tailored especially for me felt like a triumph, but after only one quarter at Lone Mountain College, which had been established in 1898, the school closed down without any warning. It is now a part of the University of San Francisco. My plan had failed and I felt lost and defeated. Mom and Dad did not give me any guidance because they did not know anything about going to college.

Since I had already made the move to San Francisco, I decided that the most sensible thing to do would be to go to SF State University. It was a much bigger, more impersonal institution than picturesque, intimate Lone Mountain College that I had hoped would be my anchor for the next four years. That September, I began working toward a very challenging double major in both psychology and dance. SF State was a much bigger school, and I could not really follow the education plan that had been set up to be achieved at a much smaller college with a dance department. At SF State, dance was in the PE department, and it was not clear which courses I needed to take.

When my family came back from Europe, I tried to explain all the changes I had gone through since they had left to go on location. I had to ask my parents for financial help. I never even considered applying for any kind of scholarship. I figured without ever looking into it that, with a father who was a famed TV star, I would never qualify for assistance anyway. I felt embarrassed about giving Mom and Dad the details of what college would cost. I was just learning day by day how much I would have to pay for rent, books, and tuition. I had no idea of how to make a budget. We had never talked about these things. Instead, my parents often reminded me that Mary and Richard had been tough on Dad when he was starting out as an actor and that their toughness had forced him to make it on his own.

Dad was often very generous with me. He paid for the private high school I really wanted to attend and had bought me a secondhand car. He also paid for dance class and dance therapy. But he did not seem to be very pleased that I would be living so far from home. Whenever I came back for a visit, he did all he could to convince me to stay. Dad had his priorities, and paying for college was not high on his personal list. I lived on a couple of hundred dollars a month. I rented a cheap ground-floor studio in Haight-Ashbury, a neighborhood our family had visited during the 1967 Summer of Love. I had fond memories of the place, but by 1976, the bright colors had faded, and there were a lot of junkies and drunks hanging around. Ever optimistic, I tried to bring my little place back to its former glory by painting murals on my walls and putting pots of flowers in the windows. I was careful with whatever money Dad sent me, but I also worked a few jobs to support myself. On weekends, I had a job as a life model for drawing classes at the Academy of Art University; on weekday afternoons I worked in the student union. Fortunately for me, most students did not like the lentil soup the management insisted we serve at the cafeteria, so I always had leftover food to take home for the weekend. Just like Dad had done, I was stuffing dinner rolls into my pockets, scrounging free food wherever I could find it.

When I came home to visit, I was transported to a different world: Dad would pull up at the airport to meet me in his custom-built dark-brown delivery van with its dome skylight and king-size bed. I'd be completely worn out from the long hours at work while trying to keep up with my studies. The Rolling Stones would be blaring out of sliding doors as he threw them open for me, and the pungent smell of marijuana would engulf me as I entered. Dad would give me a big hug and pop the champagne as we pulled away from the curb. To remind me that our beach house was less than an hour away, he would already be dressed in one of the many robes my mother made for everyone in Malibu. The robe he most often chose was made of a soft brown fabric, which flowed down to his ankles and had a hood, making it look like something from a hippie monastery. He would have that expectant, giant, it's-time-to-have-fun grin on his face that assured me that home was where I should forget all my troubles; and instead everybody must get stoned.

I know that when I was at college, he missed me a lot. I still have some of the letters my folks wrote me. Mom gave me advice on how to make friends and avoid guys trying to pick me up on the street, but Dad would send me articles about attempts to legalize marijuana and little notes in which he'd quote the *Desiderata*'s dictum "Strive to be happy" or just write "I miss you, Pooh." (My name has changed many times. My given name is Heidi Christina Mary Hagman; I changed it legally to Kristina, ridding myself of Heidi and changing the spelling of Kristina to reflect my mother's Swedish heritage, but when I was a kid, Dad often called me Pooh.)

He told me more than once that he wanted me to come back home, and that may be why the financial support he gave me was so minimal. Having heard in my letters that money was tight, Ganny had gotten me work in a summer stock production of *The Sound of Music,* and working as an actress seemed a lot easier than studying for all the science prerequisites I needed for the physiology part of my degree.

My whole life changed when I stopped fighting for a college degree and dropped out of school to return to Los Angeles to go into the family business of acting. My return coincided with the beginning of *Dallas,* and my parents now had enough money to make sure I had a safe place to live close to family members while I auditioned and took acting lessons. Dad and Mom bought my aunt BB and my grandmother Helga a cottage in West Hollywood big enough to be remodeled in a way that created a studio apartment in the back with its own entrance and kitchenette for me. Dad encouraged me to seriously pursue an acting career, and he and Mom made sure I stayed on a diet and had my hair and nails done regularly. He arranged meetings for me with agents, and he got me into the Screen Actors Guild and the American Federation of Television and Radio Artists. Dad's generosity was nothing new, Bridget Fonda's mom, Susan, remembered that on my tenth birthday I impulsively said that all I wanted for my birthday was to take the piano he'd gotten me, and on which I was taking lessons, to the edge of the Grand Canyon so I could hear what it sounded like when the songs I played echoed through the canyon's massive walls. Dad said, "What a great idea! We can put it in the back of the van!" He was wildly enthusiastic about the idea of the special acoustic adventure trip and told all his friends about it, but this idea was so impractical that it didn't happen. I've never doubted that he would have done it if he could have figured out the logistics of it. Now that his little girl was at home again, he was prepared to give me whatever I needed or wanted—singing lessons, dance lessons, and acting classes.

Dad was happy: I was back in the fold.

I often wished my parents had encouraged me to stay in college, as it is one of the biggest regrets of my life that I did not continue with it. I was always aware that they did all they could to make sure I got a very unusual—and very eccentric—education. In Dad's eyes, the adventures we all had together were the best education money could buy and definitely not something for which he would ask to be forgiven. Knowing Dad, I think he would have felt a heartfelt thanks was more in order!

10

Taking Art in a New Direction

DURING THE BRIEF TIME in my life that I poured myself into the pursuit of an acting career, I was very close to Ganny and Dad. They gave me advice on how to study my lines and renewed their earlier lessons on how to pose for photographs to my best advantage. Dad saw to it that I got lots of exposure that could lead to work as an actress, like being by his side when he got his star on Hollywood Boulevard and doing talk shows on which the children of famous performers were interviewed. I had a good feel for the work and acted in the live theater without any pay but also got a few acting roles on TV and did some commercials, which paid very well.

Our dear family friend Carroll O'Connor created a character for me on his show, *Archie Bunker's Place*. I played Linda from the laundry for one season. Working on the show with Carroll gave me the opportunity to be mentored by some of the best comedic actors in the business, like Martin Balsam and Anne Meara. Carroll treated me like a member of his own family and was very patient and loving toward me.

I should have paced myself and stay focused on *Archie Bunker's Place,* but I was trying so hard to fill the footsteps of my famous grandma and Dad that, after getting up early in the morning to be on the set all day, I worked late into the night at the Comedy Store in order to get some much-needed experience in front of a live audience.

I had heard about the Comedy Store at the classes I took once a week at the Harvey Lembeck Comedy Workshop. The Comedy Store was an important and popular venue where comedic actors were given the chance to showcase their talents in front of an audience that was often packed with people from the movie and television industry. Ironically, the club was in the exact building that had once housed a nightclub called Ciro's, where my grandmother had performed in showcases as a singer in her early career. The owner of the Comedy Store, Mitzi Shore, put together groups of actors who would be on stage doing improvisations before the stand-up comedians came on. Backstage one night, I met Robin Williams, who was constantly in the news at the time because of his first big break on a show called *Mork & Mindy.* I was almost too nervous to shake hands with him, but he saw the copy of *The Catcher in the Rye* that I held under my arm and to put me at ease by making me laugh he did a hilarious five-minute riff on the book on stage later that night. Mitzi put me on as the lone woman in a group with six guys! Somehow I held my own, and I discovered the art of being the straight man (or in this case straight woman) was a lot of fun and brought some sense of reality to the improvisational sketches we did. We rehearsed at my place on the weekends and became very close both as a working team and as friends. The group included John Larroquette, Andy Garcia, Daniel McVicar, Ray Fitzpatrick, Joe Hardin, and Fred Asparagus; most of these talented men went on to have amazing careers in television, movies, and the theater, and many of them are still my very best friends today.

It would seem like I had everything a girl could wish for, but just as I saw my career laid out for me, I started developing some very self-destructive behaviors. I wasn't sleeping much, and I started to go out drinking with the guys after the show. My will to continue as a comedian came to a full and sudden stop when I became emotionally involved with one of my fellow actors. We had a very fiery affair, and at the end of an especially bad argument, I dropped him off at a rehab facility to dry out. He stayed there for a time, and when he was finished with his treatment, we separated. I had fallen so deeply for this man that when we split up, I began to drown my sorrows with more and more booze and started dating lots of different people. This was a very bad combination, and I had to do something drastic to break the cycle.

So, only eighteen months after I had come home from college, I moved away from the family again, hoping that by moving to New York I would have a chance for yet another new beginning. I went there to study the craft of acting. I wanted to work in all kinds of theater productions and not just play to get a laugh. I did not know where I was going to live, and I was sad to leave the lovely studio my mom had built for me to live in behind my aunt and Swedish grandmother. With some nostalgia, I looked back on all aspects of the crazy year and a half that I had spent in LA. I focused on any of the positive things that I had done, and the one that came most vividly to mind was the look of admiration and approval on my grandma Helga's face when I had finished a good painting. With everything else that was going on in my life then, I still painted weekly, just as I had done all through college earlier in the year. I had amassed a large enough body of good work to mount a one-person exhibition of my Georgia O'Keeffe–inspired floral paintings. My other grandmother, Ganny, helped me find a gallery in Palm Springs, and I sold almost every canvas on display. Maybe, it occurred to me, I should give up acting and paint full-time. I knew several professional artists in New York, so I intended to work with them and explore whether acting or painting was my true calling. I was just a little more than twenty years old, and I needed to find out what I was meant to do with my life.

In New York, a friend of the family helped me find a tiny, relatively cheap apartment to rent, with one window that looked out at a brick wall. I decorated my place as best I could, filling it with furniture I'd found on the streets. I painted all the street treasures periwinkle blue so the odd pieces had some kind of harmony.

I worked diligently studying acting at the HB Studio, one of the most renowned acting schools in New York, founded by Herbert Berghof. Herbert was one of the profession's most gifted and percep-tive teachers, and soon after I began studying with him, he gave me a small part in a play he was directing. I was determined not to fall into my former bad habit of drinking after the performance with the cast. Instead, I went right home on the bus, and most nights I painted until my post-performance energy had dissipated and I was finally ready for sleep. After several months of painting alone in my room, I had enough work for a one-person exhibition at a gallery on Long Island, and my self-discipline paid off in acting too; Herbert gave me a starring role in a new play at *HB Playwrights Foundation and Theatre*.

Before rehearsals started, I went back to LA for a family party. While I was back home, I went on a few dates. One of these blind dates was with a guy who must have slipped something into my drink, because I passed out, and when I awoke many hours later, I knew I had been raped. I felt dirty and defiled, and it happened in my own bedroom, right behind where my Swedish grandmother slept. Despite my loving family, I felt that LA was a dangerous place for me to live.

On the airplane back to New York, I renewed my determination to focus on work. I had started rehearsals on the play when I found out that I was pregnant. Life and art became all jumbled up for me: the play was about a girl who had run away from home and gotten pregnant. It was an emotionally demanding role that was much too close to my real life. My famous director believed Method acting, and asked me to use difficult experiences I had lived through to bring some real emotion to my character, but it was taking all the strength I had to keep my real-life tragedy separate from my acting life. While we were still in rehearsals, I decided to have an abortion. Working on the play helped me come to that conclusion because it dealt with the emotional, financial, and physical problems that a young, single woman must cope with after discovering she has an unplanned pregnancy. The theater was teaching me things that my loving father and grandmother never intended for me to learn. It was amazing that I would be doing that particular play at that juncture in my life. I was crying in the wings between acts, and though I finished the run of the play, I ultimately found that I was not cut out to live the emotionally raw life of a Method actor. My life had become a hell as I grappled with the sadness I still felt about the volatile romantic relationship I had lost back in LA and my struggles with the multitude of conflicting emotions I felt in the wake of my abortion. This was the lowest point in my life.

I had had so many bad starts in such a short frame of time that I decided I needed help to work through the intense feelings I had about ending a pregnancy and figuring out what to do next. I went to a highly recommended psychiatrist. He suggested that I was confused because there was too much going on in my life. He said, "Imagine you are in a desert with empty land around you so that you can make decisions clearly." I left his office after paying $300 for my fifty minutes and moved to the desert for a few months so that the money I had made as an actress would go further. I was not in any state to make any big decisions; I needed some time to myself. I figured in Georgia O'Keeffe country, I could paint and recover.

All during my time in New York, I had been visiting our family's dear friend Barton Benes a few times each week. We painted together in his studio. With all the other stuff I had going on, I found real solace and happiness sitting by Barton's side painting and talking. I put together a show of the watercolors I did while painting with him for a gallery on Long Island. Barton thought getting out of the city would be a good idea. He persuaded me to focus on making art. He was a very successful artist who had been fostering my talent as a painter since my early childhood. When I had accepted that demanding role in the play, he had confronted me, saying, "You can't seriously pursue art and acting. You have to choose."

At the time, I did not listen to him, but a few months later, the choice became obvious to me. Life as an artist, away from the glare of the public, was what suited me best.

The few months I had planned on spending in New Mexico turned into years. I married an artist, and though our marriage did not last, he taught me good work habits that I still make use of in my painting studio practice, and he introduced me to the supportive and thriving art community in Santa Fe. My loving parents rolled with it. They watched as I became happier and healthier surrounded by other artists under the beautiful blue skies of New Mexico. They came to visit often and eventually bought a house of their own right next door to me. They enjoyed the Santa Fe aesthetic so much that later, when they remodeled their house in Malibu, they built it in the adobe style; they even got all the rustic beams for the beach house from New Mexico.

We had great times together, hanging out with artists at the Pink Adobe restaurant and going out to Cerrillos, where I rode horses with my good friend Annie Whitney. Annie was the first person any of us knew who lived the environmentalist's dream of being completely off the grid, thanks to solar power.

I was very happy in those years. I felt at home at last, and I was making art that came from deep inside of me. Though my mother had painted when she was young, I was not trying to be like her or anyone else in my family. The comparisons of my work, with the work of the very famous people in my life, stopped. I was slowly finding my own creative spirit. I loved to be in the studio for hours on end and even got chilblains on my toes one winter as I kept painting standing in one one place long after the fire went out in the wood-burning stove. I found a deep calm inside myself that was fueled by making art.

Having struggled with the dyslexia that had always made spelling and reading so difficult for me, I had known since my early childhood that drawing and painting were my way of getting what was inside of me out onto paper. Being an optimist, Dad figured that dyslexia gave me the gift of seeing the world in a unique way and that I could translate my special vision of the world into art. Dad liked the idea of being self-taught; even before I could read, he had bought me art books with lots of illustrations by many schools of artists. His own taste in art was very eclectic: everything from the Renaissance masters to primitive artists like Ralph Fasanella, who painted New York street life; he also admired Simon Rodia, who built colorful, soaring towers out of junk in Watts, California.

Between 1983 and 1988, I had one-person exhibitions of my paintings and prints in Los Angeles, Florida, New York, and Germany, and my work was included in group shows all over the United States. In 1988, Mom and Dad bought an apartment in New York. It was in Trump Parc, a high-end apartment building on Central Park South, where their apartment had wraparound terraces and a view of Central Park. Interestingly, it was almost exactly ten blocks from my childhood apartment. Mom was having a hard time with the contractor she had hired to remodel the interior, so she asked me if I would supervise the work while she traveled with Dad. As much as I loved Santa Fe, I was a bit restless, and I thought I might try to see if I could find a gallery in New York City that would carry my work.

When I got to Trump Parc, its marble-and-brass lobby was very impressive, but the elevator did not go up to the twenty-third floor yet where my folks had their apartment. I had to walk up several flights, and the only other creatures living up that high in the building were rats that fed off the construction workers' leftover lunches. One week, I caught twenty of them. It was something of an adventure working on the remodel with the subcontractors who were installing lights and molding; when the painting crew quit, I hired some currently unemployed dancers to work with me to finish the painting. Dancers are hard workers, and they take direction well. From the beginning of this project, I knew I could not paint in the apartment, so I rented a very funky, work-only painting studio on Great Jones Street just off the Bowery for a few months. The day before I started painting there, the famous artist Jean-Michel Basquiat died of a drug overdose across the street. This was during the crack cocaine epidemic of the 1980s. Addicts would linger on the street below my studio and scream out loud in their drug-addled state. When I told Dad about this, he worried about me walking around there alone. He came to visit and went all around the neighborhood with me looking for ways to keep me safe. He pointed out alleyways I should avoid and doorways where someone might be hiding. There was a fire station on the block, so he walked in and introduced himself to all the firemen, who recognized him immediately and stopped what they were doing to give us a tour of us the firehouse. Dad promptly pulled out his specially printed "In Larry Hagman We Trust" fake hundred-dollar bills and passed them around and, in return, asked if they would watch out for me on my way to and from the studio, which they did. Dad was happy to have found a way to keep me safe. He was exploring ways to deal with all the homeless who panhandled even in his posh neighborhood, so when he walked down Central Park South he would talk to a beggar at one end of the street and show him a ten-dollar bill, then tear the bill in half and give one half to the guy. He'd say, "If you get all the other panhandlers out of my way, I will give you the other half of that bill when we get to my destination."

When Mom and Dad came to town, they would take me out shopping and buy me designer clothes. As I did when I was child, I would try them all on for Dad, and he would help me choose what to wear when I was out in public with them. The paparazzi would be omnipresent; Ron Galella took some great photos of us. Dad was determined that we were all going to look fabulous on our way into the Algonquin or the Waldorf Astoria, and he would remind us that Ganny always wanted us to find our light. Once, when they were in town for Thanksgiving, we got decked out to take a hansom cab from the Plaza Hotel to have Thanksgiving dinner with friends. We were all wrapped in the finest, most luscious furs as we were conveyed through Central Park in an open, horse-drawn carriage. It seemed to me that this was decadence personified, that nothing the fictitious Ewings did on *Dallas* would ever top what we were doing in real life. As soon as my folks left, I returned to my normal life as an artist who loved to work but who was clearly not yet famous in her own right.

My life continued to be like my childhood, with great abundance and flashes of elegance but with no stability or consistency. I found myself looking forward to the fun times with family and to working hard on my own art at all other times. It was an exciting life of extremes, but sometimes I wondered if Dad ever noticed how I lived when I was not by his side. I talked to a film writer at a party once who gave me some very good advice. He said, "Your dad's fame is not your fame, your dad's money is not your money, but your story is your story, to tell in whatever way you wish to tell it with images or words."

Looking back, I know that painting has been my primary way to tell my story. When I was growing up, my parents let me have free rein to paint on our walls. I painted huge murals, one covering our two-car garage door with images inspired by *The Chronicles of Narnia* by C. S. Lewis. I also painted a beautiful lady who was half-bird, half-woman on Dad's bathroom door. Neighbors admired these murals and hired me to paint murals for them. When I was in my teens, my work was colorful and primitive, like Peter Max, or like illustrations for the Beatles movie *The Yellow Submarine*. Childlike work of adults was popular at that time, but because my paintings were actually made by a child, their naïveté delighted the high-fashion hippie set. I painted a mural for the Malibu youth center and a few more for Bob Hope's grandchildren. My work has changed over the years, but bright, saturated color continues to play an important part of my visual identity. While he was alive, Dad's continued enthusiastic support of me as an artist was one of the few constants in my peripatetic life.

In the month before he died, I was preparing to paint a mural on his living room ceiling. We had been talking about it during the last year and planning what it should include. He wanted me to paint the midsummer sky as it looks just before sunset over the water. He was trying to bring the outside in by creating a trompe l'oeil (French for "fool the eye") experience that would make a person looking at it inside his condo feel that he or she were floating over the ocean. I had dreamed of it for months and wanted to realize his vision for him, but in the end, it became a mural I will never paint.

11

Dreaming of *Jeannie*

I N 1951, DAD TRAVELED with his mother, Richard, and their
daughter, Heller, to London, where Mary was set to star in a West
End production of *South Pacific*. Larry was turning twenty, and Mary
convinced Richard that the once-difficult boy was now a reliable young
man who had been working diligently in the theater since dropping
out of college. There was a spot in the chorus that included a small
speaking role that was, she said, just right for him. She reasoned that
it was time for her only son to understand how hard she worked. She
hoped he would see for himself what discipline it took to be the star of
a show giving a major performance eight times a week. While working in the chorus every day, he witnessed his mother up close for the
very first time in his life.

He watched how she diplomatically dealt with all the personalities
in the new London-based cast. He saw the way she worked with them
to become an ensemble that would make the show as fabulous as it
had been on Broadway. Rehearsals were grueling, and yet he saw that

she was relaxed and poised, looking *fabulous* during the many interviews and photo shoots she did for the press before the show opened. Dad still could not stand Richard, but his respect for his mother skyrocketed. Working together, they recognized something in each other: the overwhelming need to be in front of an audience. They were both actors to their cores. Richard did not have that; Mary and Richard's daughter, Heller, did not have that; no one who was ever very close to them had that. In the deepest, truest sense, they had a need to act, and it was a bond that was especially theirs. This was the only full-stage production they ever did together, and Dad often remembered it fondly. In every home we lived in, he kept an etching of the place where they'd performed, Theatre Royal, Drury Lane. It was a precious memento of their time together on that stage.

Dad's stint in *South Pacific* ended after a year, because, before he left for London, he had registered for the draft in Texas. He knew, however, that if he went back to the United States, there was a very good chance that he would see action in the Korean War. When Mary became aware of this, she did all she could to keep her son out of harm's way. *South Pacific* was the hottest ticket in London, and she made sure that Dad's military superiors and their wives came to see her in it, and though I don't know for sure, I think this might have helped Dad secure his posting in London, far from the front. Because of his theater experience, he was given the opportunity to produce, direct, and tour shows for the U.S. military stationed in Europe.

It was a job that came with a lot of responsibility, and Dad stepped up to the challenge. He had to make sure the troops got what they wanted. He was always on the hunt for good acts. His energetic, fun-loving personality was well suited to the task of going out on the town to find talent.

His four years in the military changed him. By the time they ended, he had gained a great deal of confidence and was no longer the angry, self-absorbed youth who had arrived in London as a part of his mother's entourage. Those were important years for him: he was in the cast of one of his mother's finest theater productions and then in the Special Services entertaining the troops. He had learned to deal with responsibility.

Throughout this time, Dad had no trouble dating some of the most gorgeous women in London, like Jackie Collins, but he found he was happiest when he was with Maj Axelsson, the woman he most wanted to impress and whose opinion he valued. Maj was different from other girls he had experienced; for one thing, she was not in show business. She was a well-paid clothing designer for a fashion house, talented, ambitious, and somewhat older than he was. At first, she wasn't all that interested in him; but that soon changed. Despite that, and the demands of her work, she went out with him almost every night. He impressed her with his knowledge of all different genres of music. She also liked the fact that he was able to get the best seats to any show in London. Dad said he knew it was getting serious when she decided to keep a toothbrush at his place. Eventually, she stayed at his apartment for a few months while he was on tour.

While he was away she completely remodeled Dad's bachelor pad in Saint John's Wood near Regent's Park, painting walls and sewing slipcovers for the worn-out furniture. When he came back it was Dad's turn to be impressed. She had made a home for them, which was something that all Mary's fame and money had not afforded him; he did not want to lose this woman. They were married not once but twice: first in a civil wedding and then in a church wedding with her family in attendance. He was convinced that with Maj at his side, he would make his name as an actor.

Mom and Dad arrived in New York City in 1956, a time when the city was beginning to wake up from the quiet of the postwar years and was brimming with a rebellious spirit. New York, my parents believed, had eclipsed London and Paris as the birthplace of the "new thing," in matters ranging from fashion to art exemplified by abstract expressionism. There were experiments happening on stage too, due to the proliferation of low-budget theater, which gave Dad lots of opportunity to be in front of an audience, though it did not offer much money. Over the next six years, he did about a dozen plays, many of them running only for a month; he also did several live TV shows.

Dad played all sorts of roles, from the love interest to beatniks and hustlers, but regardless of how he was costumed, there was no hiding the fact that he was very handsome, and his looks would play a part in how he was cast. Through his work he met some fine actors, like Burgess Meredith, Carroll O'Connor, and David Wayne, who remained in his life for years to come.

Mom was neither annoyed nor frightened by the fact that Dad was not making much money. She was independent, and she was resourceful. She could make things with her hands—which Dad could not do—and he admired her for it. She also had a great knack for turning whatever assets they had into cash.

She used to tell a story about a time when they didn't have enough money to get through the week. This was soon after I was born when we were living in the first apartment my parents had in New York, a small place on fabled MacDougal Street, an Italian neighborhood that was also home to the bars and clubs that were frequented by writers and artists, among them Jack Kerouac, Ernest Hemingway, Allen Ginsberg, and Jackson Pollock. Dad was in despair about money, but Mom was fearless; she had talked to the other mothers in the building who often had trouble with cash flow due to the unsteady incomes of their husbands; this was a neighborhood that watched out for its own. The women told her she could get help if she went to the local restaurant where the Italian businessmen who bankrolled most of the establishments in the area could be found at lunchtime every day. Unbeknownst to Dad, she walked down the street carrying a bag of clothes she had designed and crafted while also cradling me in her arms. She entered the restaurant, and the men sitting at the back of the place paused their meal for a moment and nodded to each other. They knew her by sight, and with that nod, she was encouraged to approach them. She respectfully asked to borrow just enough cash to pay the rent because Dad would not get a check in time from his work in the theater. She showed them examples of her expert sewing technique and told them that if she did not pay them back by the end of the month, she would make their wives something beautiful to wear.

She knew she had made a good impression, and by appealing to their ingrained respect for a mother with a newborn, she got what they needed, and Dad went to pay them back before the month was over. He told this story of Mom's ability to get the money to cover the rent many times, and I think it was a reminder to him that he never wanted to be in need like that again.

In that same year, Dad had some big successes. He finally had his Broadway debut, in a play called *Comes a Day*. He loved being on the stage, but the thing that most excited him at this point in his life was getting a role in one episode of the TV series *Harbormaster*. Working on that show caused him to recognize for the first time that TV was a medium he loved working in. He also realized it was potentially where he could make some real money for his growing family and emerge from under the immense shadow cast by his mother's talent and fame.

So he began to pursue roles on television. He appeared on numerous live television shows, including *The DuPont Show of the Month, Kraft Television Theatre,* and *Studio One.*

Over the next few years, both my parents worked like mad. Mom was designing and sewing elegant, one-of-a kind gowns day and night while Dad continued to do plays at night and, during the day, work in television and audition while continuing to take acting and singing lessons. When work was finished around 11:00 P.M., they would meet at the theater Dad was performing in, and they would often go out and socialize, which would not have been possible without Peggy as well as Mom's sister BB, who was like a second mother to me especially on those occasions when Mom needed to travel alone with Dad.

Looking back on it, there was no natural way my parents could have kept up their frenetic lifestyle. Even when I was very young, I remember them talking about taking what they called "pep pills," which is what amphetamines were often called in those days. They were popping them in their mouths the moment they felt the least bit tired, and between the pills and three packs of cigarettes a day, they were both super energetic and very fashionably thin. I have boxes filled with pictures of them taken during these early years, looking chic and in love and beautifully dressed. But it was not all glamorous. Tempers flared often, and in the midst of all this restless energy and success there was something missing; there was a fatigue under the surface and a nagging sense that life at this abnormal pace was unsustainable.

When I was three years old, a big thing happened that changed our lives. Dad got regular work on a soap opera. I remember going with Mom to watch him work on the set of *The Edge of Night*. I was always attuned to my mother's moods, and I could see how thrilled and excited she was that Dad was on television. They talked a lot about TV, about how it was going to be the next big thing. She liked that he had regular work because she was pregnant again and needed some time away from working such long hours. As much fun as they were having doing the work that both of their ambitious temperaments craved, it was hard to live in New York City on the cheap. They began to envision what a life outside of New York City could be like.

All that winter, we had been freezing in our rent-controlled apartment where the landlord kept turning off the heat in the hope that it would force us out so he could raise the rent on the next tenant. I remember going to court with Mom when she fought for our right to have heat. By then, my brother had been born, and she must have been a sympathetic vision with two young children at her side. If freezing were not enough, there was also the constant deafening rat-a-tat-tat of jackhammers because workmen were digging up the street below us to put in a new sewer system. For a household that stayed up till all hours of the night, the deafening noise at 8:00 A.M. was torture. My Swedish aunts would shake their heads and, in their lilting accents, quote the slogan displayed on billboards all over the city: "Dig we must for a growing New York."

After two years on *The Edge of Night*, my dad got his big break when he was finally cast in his first big movie role, as a serviceman in *Ensign Pulver.* It was time to get out of New York, and 1964 was a big year for Dad. The film could not have come at a better moment. It was quickly followed by *Fail Safe* with Henry Fonda, and then came *In Harm's Way* with John Wayne and Brandon de Wilde. Soon we were flying off to Rome for a film called *The Cavern.* I was so young when the film was released that I never saw it. I looked all over for a copy of it, but the most I could find was a five-minute clip on the Internet that included a short, intense performance by my father. The film was set in World War II, and as the name suggests, it took place in a cave. It could have been shot on a soundstage anywhere, but luckily for us, it was made in Europe. In it, Dad played a guy who was secretly drinking. He was good at playing drunks.

In a break from shooting *I Dream of Jeannie,* Dad was in a film in which he played a really mean drunk. It was called *The Group* and was based on the novel of the same name by Mary McCarthy. The film told the story of the loves, losses, and tribulations of eight attractive, affluent young women who knew each other from their years together at Vassar. Dad played the unscrupulous would-be theater director who marries one of the girls and hurts her so much with his ravings that she's driven to an apparent suicide. It's one of his finest performances and certainly one of his most startling portrayals. He's so out of character playing Harald Peterson in that film that most people seeing it today don't realize that my dad played Harald.

In the mid-1970s, he played a drunk again in one of his best acting roles ever, in our neighbor Paul Mazursky's film *Harry and Tonto.* The man he portrays has hit bottom and breaks down as he confesses his failure of character to his father, played wonderfully by Art Carney. I will never forget the way that performance made me feel because in his agonized admission of guilt, I saw my father being more vulnerable on film than I had ever known him to be in life.

Working on films and in TV paid a lot better than the money Dad was getting as an actor in the theater. Also there is no denying that we were all having a much better time living on location than in the apartment, where Mom worked night and day to keep us afloat. My parents decided together that it was time to move to California, the mecca of film and television, but before committing to such a big change in our lives, we all went out west for a few weeks to see if we would really like it.

Dad's good buddy Carroll O'Connor loaned us his house while he was on location. Peggy came along on this trip too, even though it meant she would have to camp out with us in a tent as we drove our Jeep across country to get there. We all loved California.

After returning to New York, my folks knew they wanted to live out west, but Dad needed to get steady work. For him, that meant getting on a show that would keep him steadily employed for years before he would take took the major step of moving the whole family away from New York. He borrowed some money for the airfare to Los Angeles, where he planned to audition for a number of roles while staying with his old high school friend Ted Flicker, who had become a successful director and writer.

Mom had to stay in New York City, where she continued to make dresses to support the family. She hated being away from Dad and never seemed to get any sleep. She was constantly working. She designed, cut, and sewed the most beautiful and glamorous gowns for performers like Jane Morgan and Sophie Tucker, people my parents met through Mary and Richard.

Jane Morgan was Mom's best client. Mom made so many outfits for her that we had a dress designer's dummy in our house that had been padded to be an exact replica of Morgan's body. That way the singer did not have to be present for hours of fittings.

Mom took me with her to buy fabric, an easy walk from our apartment on West Forty-Ninth Street. All the guys at the fabric store knew my mother; we were regulars. They must have been good family men because rather than being annoyed that a patron had brought a child along, they knew how to make me feel comfortable. They would seat me at the very top of the stepladder and cut bright-colored swatches of fabric for me to hold. From my vantage point, I could see my mother walk all over the place getting inspiration for new designs by looking at the multitude of colors and textures of these gorgeous fabrics. There were bolts and bolts of fabric stacked high to the ceiling; she would ask the assistant to bring down any bolt that caught her eye and seemed to be worth a closer inspection. The big, strong assistants would climb up to the top of the stacks and shoulder the heavy bolts to bring them to where my mother stood beside a tall cutting table. Then they would unfurl the fabric dramatically from the bolt so we could see how it would catch the light and move. Mom taught me how to rub the fabric between my thumb and index fingers and analyze what the piece was made of. I would close my eyes and feel the texture and weight of the material. Mom and the salesmen taught me the different characteristics of finely woven silk as contrasted with heavy wool fabrics woven into a herringbone pattern. They taught me the difference between muslin and polished chintz and how to tell if lining fabric was synthetic by the way it felt and the way it smelled.

These experienced salesmen enjoyed having a buyer in their store who understood their product as well as my mother did. She would have them cut samples so she could take them home to inspire her and help her decide which material to invest in for an outfit or gown. She knew how to bargain with them, because the price of the material would cut into her profit, but she was respectful of paying the right price for good quality. As young as I was, I admired my mom and her interactions with these men. She was a fine businesswoman.

Mom always had deadlines to meet. Jane Morgan was mercurial and seemed to want a new gown for a show at the very last minute, and making it that quickly was always a challenge, since Mom did everything herself. She said her pep pills would keep her awake so she could get the work done; she was edgy with Dad gone. She turned our dining room, which was big by New York standards, into a studio. I still had the habit of seeking out my parents when I woke from a nightmare, and one night I went looking for Mom, who was still at work. The dining room/studio floor was completely covered in shimmering bright-red silk organza for a gown that, according to the sketches Mom had made, would be cut on the bias and trail out behind the singer as she walked on stage. In my half-asleep state, I was really worried about Mom; she looked so tired, trapped behind all that red.

I wanted to go to her, but as I approached, she yelled at me and told me not to come anywhere near the precious fabric. It was an unforgettable image: my mother at the far end of the room behind a sea of smooth red fabric with hundreds of shiny, sharp silver pins in it. I felt the need to comfort her, but I was a helpless child. I wanted to grow up fast so I could take care of her.

At last there was good news from LA. Dad had done a screen test for a new show called *I Dream of Jeannie*. He was well aware that our family desperately needed a change, and in his wildly optimistic way, even before he knew whether or not he had gotten the job, he rented a little cottage in Santa Monica Canyon, just three blocks from the beach. Soon after that, we learned that he had been cast in his first leading role in a television series. We were all overjoyed and relieved! Mom had been working so hard, and everyone in our whole household had been completely focused on this goal. Now Dad had what he'd always wanted.

When he came back to New York, we packed up and piled into the station wagon bought with profits from my mother's dress designing and drove across the country. I was excited to go, but as we got farther and farther from New York I was sad that my aunts BB and Lillimor and my babysitter, Peggy, were all staying in the city. The one upside to this was that, for several years, my aunts kept the rent-controlled apartment in New York, so I was able to retain a connection to the life and place that were familiar to me.

As we drove through the South, Mom was very outspoken about the discrimination she saw. She had grown up in Sweden and had very little experience with African Americans or the horrible way they were often treated in America. She chastised a young white man at a café who called an older black man "boy." As she did this, everyone in the place went silent. Quickly, Dad knew how tense things could get in the South and hustled us all out to the station wagon. Mom was fearless and indignant and wanted to change things right there and then, but Dad knew she could put us all in danger, and he was not about to be the lone man defending his outspoken foreign wife. Dad was well aware that, in 1964, bad things happened to folks in the South who stood up against racial inequality.

I've always regarded this story as being less about my mother's politics and more about what a loose cannon she was. She was reckless and fearless; in the story as Dad told it, she had even had the courage to contact the Mafia to get rent money. Sadly this story is the forerunner of things that would happen as Alzheimer's took her over, and she became the uncontrollable person who hit her caretakers.

But on that particular day, no one thought too much more about it; we were focused on moving along down the road to our new life.

My very first memory of Los Angeles was of Dad driving us into Santa Monica Canyon and my being awakened by the lush scents of night-blooming jasmine and orange blossoms that were carried by the warm, caressing Santa Ana winds and wafting through our station wagon's windows. If this was any indication of what our new life in California was going to be like, our move was truly going to be wonderful.

The trip across the country had been so exciting that after a while I had forgotten that I was leaving my aunts and Peggy behind. I had more time with my parents than I could ever remember having, and I loved it. They kept commenting on the weather and how great everything was going to be now that we had moved away from the gray, cold, crowded city.

The culture out west was really different. In Manhattan, disparities in class structure were totally visible and literally walking distance apart: certain neighborhoods had doormen out front of elegant buildings, and then you could walk a few blocks and get to a neighborhood like ours, where prostitutes hung out in the doorways. On the Upper East Side, all the kids wore uniforms, while on my street, they wore mismatched hand-me-downs. In California, the class disparity was hidden from view because the poor areas of town were miles away from the middle- and upper-class enclaves. As a child living in a nice neighborhood I seldom noticed anyone in need.

Behavior was very different too, out by the beach where we lived in a wooden house in the shade of Santa Monica Canyon. The people around us seemed naturally fit; they even walked differently from New Yorkers. No one seemed to be in a rush to get anywhere, and they all dressed so casually as if comfort were much more important than conformity. It was like all the rules about style and comportment were discarded. Mom, who was always so aware of fashion, was taking note of the body consciousness that did not include girdles or bras. Everything was so different from New York, much freer, warmer, much more colorful, less bound in tradition.

The LA fixation on healthy living and hard bodies was contagious. Dad stopped smoking cigarettes and began working out. When I look at the old *Jeannie* episodes I'm always struck by how slim and great looking he was then. During our first year in LA, my parents continued to take the pep pills that had made them so energetic in New York, but finally their prescriptions ran out. Mom was really angry when she went to refill it and the pharmacist refused to give her any more pills. A law had been passed prohibiting the sale of the drug Bontril, because it was habit forming. At first Dad was pissed off too—"What a lot of bullshit!"—but it engendered one of those aha! moments because it forced them to face the fact that they had been addicted to amphetamines. But getting off the drug wasn't easy. Dad had a hard time keeping his temper on the set, and Mom was grumpy and constantly dieting, which for her meant eating practically nothing. Dieting was an obsession for both of them.

I was a chubby kid, and Mom had always tried to restrict what I ate, but back in New York, Peggy was the one who had fed me. Mom used to get mad at her when she found out that she was taking me to the cafeteria at the zoo to have french fries and burgers. Now Mom was in control of mealtime, and I was always hungry and sneaking food when she wasn't looking. Sometimes Mom just wouldn't cook, and when Dad came home there would be nothing to eat, so we'd walk to the Golden Bull restaurant just down the street and right across the Pacific Coast Highway from the beach. Mom was virtually starving herself and one night she passed out at the table. I remember being worried about her, but Dad distracted us by getting Preston to imagine what kind of wife he was going to have when he grew up. Preston said his wife would have twenty children and eat whole bottles of ketchup every day. It was such an odd, fanciful story that I never forgot it or the evening that my brother told it to us.

I loved to sit and watch TV as soon as I got home from school. Dad was serious about limiting the amount of TV we kids could watch, and he became even more aware of the powerful effects of TV viewing after reading Marshall McLuhan's new book *Understanding Media*, which came out in 1964 when I was six. In New York, the issue of how much time I could spend watching TV was pretty much taken care of because Ganny had made sure I was sent to one of the best schools in the city, and she also gave us memberships to all the museums. The school, the *École Française*, had strict guidelines about the cultural things children should be exposed to. My routine consisted of being picked up at school, where we wore cute little gingham uniforms, and being taken by Peggy to a museum, which also kept me out of the apartment, where Mom had to work.

But in Los Angeles, I was much more on my own, and I would walk home alone and then plop down on the floor and turn on the TV. Dad was at work all day, and Mom was often grumpy, so she didn't want to be bothered and didn't stop me. I had trouble making friends, and watching TV was a lot easier than trying to fit in with new kids in this strange town. I loved shows like *Gilligan's Island* and *Bewitched*. They were silly, make-believe shows perfect for a kid to veg out with, and they had begun the year before *I Dream of Jeannie*, so they could be seen in reruns in the afternoon after school.

Like those shows, *I Dream of Jeannie* was fanciful and magical. It was the story of a young man, an astronaut named Tony Nelson, played by Dad, who discovered a beautiful young woman who happened to be a genie who constantly surprised him with her unabashed passion and the ability to grant him his every wish.

Dad's show came on once a week in the evening, and he made us watch it in silence. We could not say a word until the commercials came on. Watching the show was very serious business for Dad, but he loved it when we giggled.

He was always thinking about how to make it better. He often had friends over to watch with us, and they would have intense discussions about how the show could be improved. Still, in the early years of *I Dream of Jeannie*, Dad was ecstatic. His mother had always been such a big star; her pictures were often on the covers of magazines, but now he was on the cover of *TV Guide*, and he was thrilled about it.

His mother's work had set a daunting challenge for him. He had so much admiration for her talent, dedication, and hard work. He was determined to be as good in television as she had been in the theater. To achieve this, he would have to equal her skill and perfectionism.

Mary had worked with Broadway's most gifted writers and composers: Cole Porter, Richard Rodgers, Oscar Hammerstein, Adolph Green, Betty Comden, and Jule Styne. They were all dedicated to their craft and would rehearse for countless hours until every number in the show was brilliant.

Dad wanted to do everything in his power to make his show the best show on TV. But unlike the musicals my grandmother worked in, where, after an opening on Broadway, she had the exact same script for every performance, Dad had to work with a new script each week, for every one of the 139 episodes of *I Dream of Jeannie*. This meant he had very little time to make things as fantastic as he needed them to be. On top of that, he was always in the shadow of the enchanting woman who played Jeannie, the beautiful Barbara Eden. Dad seldom talked about his costar to us; he was respectful of her but rarely consulted her about the show to my knowledge.

I tried to understand something about their relationship by binge watching *I Dream of Jeannie* episodes one day, while I was writing this book. The premise of the show was that Jeannie was Tony's fantasy, but it looked like there was true affection between Tony and Jeannie, and I noted that their kisses were very warm and that she was genuinely affectionate as was his response. Barbara's character never fought with Dad's character: she just threw her arms around him and covered him with kisses till he shut up.

Dad was always asking the writers and producers for better scripts, but when he got the same story line over and over again, he began meeting with two of the other actors—Bill Daily and Hayden Rorke—to come up with new lines and sight gags.

At times, Dad even went so far as to completely change all aspects of a scene. For example, if Jeannie blinked her master, Tony Nelson, back into the spaceship after he insisted he really did want to go to the moon, he would land back in the capsule upside down. He was always doing pratfalls: tumbling downstairs or over the back of the couch; he never wanted to just walk and talk—there had to be lots of movement. He took his cue from silent Buster Keaton films. He brought a lot of physical comedy to *Jeannie;* maybe that's why the show has been so successful in so many foreign countries.

No matter what he was working on, Dad left nothing to chance. I remember crawling all over a set with him one day, feeling the floor with our hands to make sure no nails or stray pieces of glass would be in the path of his stunt. All these pratfalls took a lot more time than playing it straight. But he loved making people laugh. He thought about the show night and day and always felt the pressure to be funnier and sharper than he'd been before. Like his mom, he came alive when people were watching him, but at home, we could see that he had moments of deep insecurity and doubt; for such a fun guy, he worried a lot.

In the past, he had smoked to calm his nerves, smoking as many as three packs of cigarettes a day. Now he calmed himself by smoking a lot of pot instead. His wide, glazed-eyed grin did not always jibe with what was going on around him. With his flowered peasant shirts and rose-colored glasses, my costume-loving father felt right at home in an era when colorful and shockingly unexpected clothes were the fashion. He put his outfits together with the same care that his mother or Richard would for a public appearance, but unlike them—whose mutual goal was to be glamorous—his goal was to flout convention.

He tried to get his mother to smoke pot with him. He had a thing for getting older people to try it, and he would watch how they reacted to the drug. He always wanted to turn people on, but Mary thought it was bad for him. His insistence that she try pot upset her, and she made that very clear in a letter she wrote him. "I don't approve of your life," it read. "The world is full of revolt and you are at the head of the class. Are you so insecure in your work? You become a better actor through performing. Not with the help of pot."

Watching *Jeannie* every week with Dad and being on the set to see how the show was made was something like being backstage when we lived in New York. I came to know the show very well. I was really proud of my dad in his role as the astronaut Captain Tony Nelson. Even as a kid, I knew the country was caught up in a fascination with going beyond our planet and landing on the moon. What could be better than having your dad play a space hero? But the country was at war in Vietnam, and astronauts are also members of the air force. When *Jeannie* debuted in 1965, it was a time when U.S. airmen were being shot down and killed in Vietnam. Though he had been in the air force himself during the Korean War, Dad was vehemently against the Vietnam War, so playing Captain Nelson was sometimes uncomfortable for him.

He had been taking me to peace marches, and he wore a peace symbol around his neck and talked a lot about conscientious objectors who were fleeing to Canada or going to jail because they opposed the war and refused to fight. Though Ganny went to Vietnam performing *Hello, Dolly!* for the troops, Dad didn't do shows for servicemen; he admired men who fought for their country, but he silently protested the war by trying not to be identified with the military during what he believed to be an unjust war.

But one day, the whole family stopped in at an air force base where Dad was going to do an informal autograph signing. It was right on our way to the foothills of Yosemite where Dad's fellow actor on *Jeannie,* Barton MacLane, who played the general, had a ranch where we often stayed. At the base, a picnic was in progress in the midst of a housing facility where servicemen's families lived. The crowd was made up of wives, mothers, and children. There were very few men; nearly all of them were away in combat.

A boy just about my age came up to me. He told me that my dad was his dad too. This was confusing to me and made me grumpy. I complained to Dad, saying, "I'm your little girl. I know this boy can't be your son."

Dad patiently sat me down and explained that the boy had not seen his father for months because he was far away in the war. He told me, "When I am Tony Nelson wearing my uniform, I look just like his dad. The TV brings me into his living room every week, so while his own dad cannot get home, he needs me to be his dad. You have to share today."

With me by his side, Dad went to hug this little boy, and we all walked around the compound together. The boy was so happy, and the way his sad face brightened had a huge effect on Dad. I think he may have had an epiphany that day about his ability to make a difference in people's lives, and he helped me understand his responsibility to everyone who supported our family by watching him on television. From that day on, I understood that my father would never be mine alone; he belonged to his public.

12

LSD Trips of Another Kind

WITH *DALLAS* DAD EVENTUALLY PROVED he had what it took to mold a show into something everyone would be riveted by. But his determination to perfect *I Dream of Jeannie* and make it the best show on television almost ruined him. Between his constant complaints to the producers about bad scripts and his erratic behavior due to amphetamine withdrawal and pot smoking, things eventually, and perhaps inevitably, spun out of control. I didn't understand what really happened at the end of *Jeannie* until years later when I read, in Dad's own words, about how he had gone berserk on the set. It happened when the show was in its fifth year. One of those endless rehearsals that Dad insisted on was taking place on a particularly hot day. The air conditioner on the set was so loud the actors couldn't hear each other's lines. Dad asked the technicians to turn it off. When they didn't, he repeated his request and then repeated it again. When they still did nothing, he stormed over to where the fire retardant and an axe hung on the wall, then picked up the axe and pounded it into a giant cord. Everything went dark. He'd meant to shut off the air conditioners; instead he'd cut the cord that supplied electricity to the entire soundstage. When the lights went out, he knew he had blown it. Working on *Jeannie* was never the same after that day. He was afraid he would never work again; he knew he had gone way too far.

His then best friend, Ted Flicker, who directed some episodes of *Jeannie,* insisted that Dad see a psychiatrist who could help him get things into perspective. Dad agreed even though he was never interested in talking about his problems. As Dad always told it, after a few sessions, the psychiatrist told him he needed to see that he had an amazing life and then suggested he take LSD. It's another one of Dad's stories that may or may not be true. I've often thought he was curious about LSD and more comfortable with the idea of experimenting with it if the green light for doing so came from his therapist.

Right about this time, Dad's friend Peter Fonda took him to a Crosby, Stills, and Nash concert and afterward took him backstage where he met David Crosby, who gave him some very high-quality LSD.

Having read *The Joyous Cosmology,* Dad hoped that LSD would open the door to enlightenment. Talk therapy was not going to take him where he wanted to go. And so he turned to LSD to help him allay his anxieties and find that always-elusive balance between work and life.

Over the next few weeks, Dad proceeded to get ready to take his first trip. Unlike many people at the time who were dropping acid casually, my father planned this trip as carefully as he prepared to do a pratfall on the set. He talked to a lot of people who had taken LSD and one of them was a friend of his from their high school days back in Weatherford, Texas, who was now living in LA and had gone on many hallucinogenic trips. Larry Hall was the quintessential hippie; he had long dark hair and dressed in fringed buckskins and looked sort of like a Native American. He offered to be my father's Virgil and lead him to the unknown world of LSD and safely bring him out again. They planned a quiet, safe environment for Dad's first trip. Mom was part of the plan too and arranged to take me and my brother out for the whole day so the men would be free from the distractions of the family.

It turned out to be an amazing experience in which Dad explored what happens to us when we die. During the trip he felt connected to his beloved grandmother, whose death had been one of the most frightening experiences of his life. After the trip he continued to feel her presence in his life.

My dad would never refer to an afterlife as heaven. We had no religion. Mom's family had been very strict Lutherans back in Sweden, and she had hated church. Dad's peripatetic life had never included going to church, and I was brought up being told by my parents that religion was invented to control the masses. Their attitude was: if you believed in heaven and hell, you were a fool.

I developed my own beliefs, and after Dad died, I read a lot of books that described people's deathbed or near-death experiences. There was a common theme among them that begins with the feeling of being afraid at an entrance of some kind, a gate or the opening to a tunnel or a cave; beyond the entrance, a bright light can be seen in the distance. People who have religion call this place heaven, but people like my dad, who want to eschew the notion of a heaven that is beyond this world, struggle to describe it. This is how my dad wrote in his book about his LSD vision of what I would call heaven:

"Suddenly I saw the entrance to a cave across the room. It was guarded by octopuslike creatures with long writhing tentacles. There were also two other creatures that looked like lions with feathers. Then I turned and saw my grandmother, who'd died when I was *twelve. She was to my left, hovering about eight feet above me. She sat in the same position I was in, and wore the same robe. She didn't speak or motion. She simply looked at me with a wonderful, comforting smile and told me not to worry about it."* As his trip continued, he was sucked into a tunnel at incredible speed. A voice told him to go with it. At the end of this tunnel he saw a bright light.

Over the course of our lives together, he repeatedly told me that this LSD vision of his grandmother welcoming him at the entrance of, whatever you want to call it, had taken his fear of death away. If there was another plane of existence after this life, she was surely there, and if she were there, death would be like going home.

He was so excited about what he had learned on his trip that he wanted to share it with my mother so that she too could experience it. He wanted her to have the same spiritual awakening he felt he had had.

It was not until a year later that Mom and Dad took acid together. She was not into pot in the way that he was, but he liked getting stoned with her. They had always been partners and playmates, and though she hadn't embraced the hippie culture as much as Dad had, he really wanted her to experience the revelations that LSD had given him.

Dad had always thought Mom was beautiful and sexy, but she had been insecure about her appearance since contracting polio in her early twenties, which had left her face a bit paralyzed on one side. I thought it gave her a lovely crooked smile, which I emulated. Still, no matter how many times Dad told her she was beautiful, she didn't believe it, and naturally, that frustrated him. As it turned out, it was during the acid trip she took with him that she turned to Dad and suddenly said, "I'm beautiful."

Dad said, "I've been trying to tell you that for years."

Tripping together was so bonding for them that they decided they needed some more time alone. Dad suggested they go off to Montreal where they were already beginning to put up new experimental buildings in preparation for Expo 67. Mom had always been fascinated by architecture, and Dad wanted her to explore her creative side that she really hadn't utilized since she'd stopped designing clothes when we moved to LA.

When we lived in New York City, they had been able to go away alone frequently because Mom's sisters and Peggy were there to care for my brother and me, but now they did not have that safety net. Since we were still pretty new to the LA area, they did not know a network of families who could recommend reliable babysitters. Mom did not know of anyone who would be willing to be responsible for two young kids for an entire week, and in the absence of that individual their plan was going to fall apart. My father never liked the idea of hiring people to take care of kids, but now he missed having BB and Peggy around. He felt he really needed some time alone with his wife, so he turned to Larry Hall, who was not working at the time and had, after all, guided Dad safely on his initial LSD journey. It did not occur to him that taking care of children was serious business and that this single man who was not responsible enough to have a job and who got high all the time might not be the best babysitter.

While Dad was exploring his inner world, I was discovering that my life in Santa Monica was completely different from my previous life. In New York Peggy held my hand and walked me to a little school on the Upper West Side where I wore a pink gingham uniform. Once there I made art and sang songs and learned poems all in French. Ganny thought it would be so chic for me to be in a French emersion school. In New York I was never allowed to go anywhere without an adult, but in Santa Monica all the kids walked to school on their own. During the first month at school the reality that I could not read became very evident to me. Everyone else seemed to be able to read the adventures of Dick and Jane but it was not in French. I did not have my foreign teachers smiling at me with understanding nods because of course the little American could not be expected to read in French yet. I did not know what was wrong with me. A year later I was tested and began to get help with dyslexia but during these first weeks I was lost. I had arrived in my new school just when everyone was taking the Iowa Tests for Basic Skills. I could not read the instructions and I just sat looking at the paper. The teacher kept me after class thinking I was just being stubborn but after watching me sit for an hour silently crying she finally let me go. I had to go to the bathroom but I raced out of the school building not wanting to be in that horrible place for one minute longer. I hid behind a bush to relieve myself but I had not noticed that a group of girls had been following me to taunt me for being kept behind after everyone else went home. They had seen me in the bushes and started teasing me and kicking me. I crouched down to protect myself, and I started to cry again. They kept telling me how gross I was for peeing in public. I did not know it was bad to pee behind a bush; I had done it often when we were driving across the country, and Mom and Dad had told me to do it when we pulled off the road. When I got home I told Mom about it, and she said what I had done was perfectly natural, but it was not a good idea to pee on the way home from school. After that, I stopped talking to the girls at school. I was sad and lonely much of the time during my first few months in California despite the beautiful weather and all the trees and lovely flowers in our neighborhood. Finally I did make friends with a nice girl who lived close by, but she had violin lessons a few times a week, so I was still on my own a lot.

There was a boy in my class, Jimmy, whose really short hair made his ears look like they stuck straight out at right angles from his head. He lived down the street from us in a house that I passed every day on the way to and from school. He had several brothers, and his mom ran a day care center at their home. One day, he started talking to me as we were walking the same way, and soon, we began to play on many afternoons in the vacant lot between our houses. There was a big oak tree that we climbed. He showed me that there was a secret hiding place behind the back wall of our garden where it was dark and thick with foliage. There was lots of debris to make pretend houses with. After building our wobbly structure, we pretended that we were the mother and father of our new home.

At the start of the week that Larry Hall was supposed to be taking care of us, I walked home from school alone and found a strange, long-haired teenage boy in my backyard. He was sitting cross-legged and wouldn't respond when I spoke to him. Larry explained that the boy was too high to talk to me. I did not really understand why he was at our house; he was too young to be Larry Hall's friend and too old to be a playmate for me or Preston. I had not seen people as stoned as that before.

Memory is fallible. When any given group of people experiences a particular event, each person will remember it in a different way. Memory is especially fragile when it comes to recalling something that frightened you; those are the moments that can be the most difficult to remember clearly and the hardest to completely forget.

A day or two after the long-haired guy was at our house, Larry took me to my Brownies meeting. There was a special ceremony that day about crossing a bridge that was meant to signify my transformation from a Brownie to a full-fledged Girl Scout (a young woman with purpose). I was excited to think of myself as growing up and being good and taking on more responsibility.

I have a picture of myself that Larry took of me in my new uniform when I had just been initiated as a budding Girl Scout. I was a chubby little girl with thick, blond, blunt-cut bangs, looking shyly at Larry behind the camera. When I look at that picture, I always think that it had captured the last moment in my life when I was totally innocent.

The day after it was taken, I came home from school, and Larry was not there. Instead, there were three teenage boys in my room; one of them was Jimmy's older brother. I remember that they had a big bowl of tomatoes and a baseball bat. Jimmy climbed up to the top of the bunk beds my brother and I shared. He squished the tomatoes in his hands, sending their pulp and seeds flying all over the ceiling. At first I thought this was some strange game they were playing. I told him my mother would be mad and he should not do that. But then his big brother smashed the baseball bat against the wall and said, "Your head is going to look like those tomatoes if you don't do exactly what I tell you to do."

I remember them laughing at me and one big boy taking his pants off. He got on the floor, and I could see his penis standing up. I remember protesting that I did not like it, and that was when the big boy told me what a bad girl I was. He said everybody knew I did bad things; I peed outside and played with boys. He got louder and said that if I did not do everything he told me to do, he would make sure everyone at school and Girl Scouts knew I was a bad girl. I remember that my clothes were off, but how they came off is something I don't remember . . . I remember being on the floor looking at his penis with all the other boys around me. He told me to lick him. I didn't want to, but I did it. I licked him just the way he told me to do. I felt guilty, wrong, dirty, bad.

When they were leaving, the big boy who had had his pants off said he would know if I said a word to anyone, and he would come back into my house and tell my parents what a bad girl I was, and then they would not want me anymore.

When the door closed, I saw tomato stains on the ceiling. For months I saw them when I climbed up to my top bunk; each time I saw them, I thought again about that terrifying afternoon. In the morning, the first thing I saw was those tomato stains on the ceiling, and I would remember again that my own bedroom was not a safe place to be.

For weeks following that event, I had horrible headaches that came on every day as I walked home from school. I spent even more time alone than I had before, watching TV and drawing pictures. I felt even more distant from the other kids at school. I felt they could tell that I was different. I tried to hide in my bed every night, afraid the boys would sneak in to my room again when everyone was asleep. I slept with the covers pulled over my head, thinking if I could be perfectly, perfectly still, no one could see I was in the room. To be as still as possible, I held my breath; sometimes I held it until I passed out. I was afraid to tell my parents what happened because they would think I was not their good little girl. I felt so alone.

Not long afterward, we moved to Malibu. My violin-playing friend, Sarah, came out to our new house for a sleepover, and I told her what happened. As will happen when kids move far apart, I did not see Sarah much after that, but I also thought maybe she did not like me after I told her, and that reinforced the idea that I should not tell anyone ever.

When I was an adult, I tried to look Sarah up, shyly leaving notes at her house, but I never found her. Having moved back to my same neighborhood in Santa Monica as I was writing this book, I ran into a very old couple who looked like her parents. They walked every day on the bluffs that overlook the ocean just as I had made the habit of doing. Each time I saw them, I wanted to stop them and ask about Sarah, but I thought I might frighten them. In a strange series of coincidences, I finally found her through a contractor I'd hired to do some work at my home. He told me that his sister and I had been in my same grade elementary school. I had coffee with her. She remembered Sarah and found her on the Internet and connected us. All the fears I had been carrying around since my childhood, that she would shun me, melted away. She was now a science professor in a city a few hours away, and she was coming to town in a week or so, and she suggested we meet at her parents' house. The house was exactly as it had been when I was a kid. Few things in life stay the same, and this part of my childhood, which had been so difficult to remember, had physical form in the familiarity I felt as I walked through Sarah's door. We sat at their dining table and had coffee and muffins. I told them I was writing a book and how hard it was to remember details about the past. I did not want to talk about my shame and the incident I had shared with Sarah so many years ago at our sleepover in Malibu; I could not even hint at it in front of her family, but when we were alone in the kitchen together, she brought up the fact that her older brother said that some of the older boys in the neighborhood back then had been mean bullies. In that moment, I finally felt someone knew what I knew. It was like having a fact check of what I'd always known.

Even at that time, so many years later, whenever I thought of that awful day, I wished there had been a grown-up there to protect me. I blamed Larry Hall for not making sure I was safe. Ironically, he came to visit me after my first child was born, and he brought her a carved wooden Native-American totem of a mother protector to hang over her crib. The gift prompted me to say something to Larry. I asked him if he had any idea of what had happened to me while I was in his care back in the house in Santa Monica. He stared at me blankly. I don't know if his expression said, "No, I don't know," or "I know, and I am not going to say anything unless you do," or if it simply meant, "Uh-oh. What happened while I was too stoned to notice?" So I told him everything I could, only what I clearly remembered, and he seemed sad about it and apologized. The apology was like a soothing balm that I needed to hear. It helped me let go of a lot of anger.

That sense that my home was not a safe place was a feeling I held inside me as long as I lived at home with my parents, and it may be something that few would understand. Most people thought that living in our Malibu house was utopian. When guests arrived, they found the Jacuzzi, lots of wine, music, and food, and a happy family. Most of the time, that illusion was also the truth; as chaotic as our family existence often was, my parents, with the help of my mother's sisters, created a warm home life. Still, there were some people who misunderstood that even our freewheeling lifestyle had its limits. These were people who failed to recognize that being naked in our Jacuzzi did not give them a license to have sex with everyone they laid their eyes on. People roamed around the house at all times of the day and night, and as I approached puberty, I learned to tell drunk and stoned men of every kind to get out of my room.

Because Dad talked openly about his belief that drugs connected a person to their higher consciousness, our home got a reputation for being a place where people came to take psychedelic drugs, and it was known to be a safe place to come down from a trip if things were feeling too strange. But I knew the dangerous place our open home could be at times when my aunts or my parents were not there. And my fears of an unwelcome visitor forcing me to do things against my will again came true many years after we left the little house in Santa Monica, where the boys had traumatized me.

I still struggle to unravel fact from fiction about this story too. I've gone over it time and time again. I have heard my father retell this story of Dennis Hopper misbehaving in our home with many variations and his own embroideries and additions. I have my own version of what happened; my memories are harsh and consistent.

My parents went out of town for a week. I was just fifteen, and my brother was eleven. My folks rightly thought we were too young to be alone, so an old friend of the family, John, stayed at the house with us. We had known John since our days in Sterling Forest; he was the son of John Houser. He had become a regular at our house, and after Dad had been stopped several times by the highway patrol and been tested for drunk driving, he figured that the odds were against him and that the next time he was stopped he could lose his license and the publicity would cost him work, so Dad hired John to drive him to and from work every day. Having a driver meant Dad could be comfortable drinking throughout the workday knowing he could relax all the way home to Malibu. Dad didn't think anything of the fact that John was often stoned; pot driving was not the same as drunk driving. John was a nice guy, but he was not the kind of guy who knew anything about taking care of children. Again, Dad had chosen the wrong person to watch over my little brother and me.

On one of the afternoons while my folks were out of town, Dennis Hopper came over uninvited. We had known him for quite a while, as he was part of Peter Fonda's network of friends. He walked right into

the house as if he belonged there, though our family had not social-
ized with him in years. The last time I had seen him was during one
of our many camping trips across America in the summer of 1970.
That summer, Dennis was holed up in Taos, New Mexico, editing a
film in an amazing historic home that had been owned by the renowned arts patron Mabel Dodge Luhan. Dad was curious to see him
in this interesting setting, and he also wanted to see some of *The Last
Movie*, which Dennis was working on and which was said by everyone
to be a masterpiece. Mom was uncomfortable about the visit, but Dad
was not going to pass up the adventure. *Easy Rider* had made Dennis
a counterculture icon, and bikers from all over America were making
pilgrimages to Taos to see their hero. Dad did not have a motorcycle
himself at that time, but he was very interested in the lifestyle of these
folks. We drove through the beautiful countryside till we got to a big,
run-down, old adobe home. It was interesting, but I picked up on Mom's
uneasy vibe, and I was very uncomfortable. There was too much male
energy, and everyone, including Dad, was stoned and drunk; no matter
how happy everyone seemed, there was a menacing undercurrent, a
sense that things could sour or go off the rails at any minute. *The Last
Movie* had been shot in Peru, and after seeing some of the footage,
Mom called the movie a hundred-pound–cocaine film, meaning it
only looked good after snorting a hundred pounds of cocaine.

The loud and unruly behavior of the bikers increasingly frightened
me. I was relieved when we left New Mexico. And although Dennis
and his film were frequent subjects of conversation among Dad's
friends, I don't remember seeing him again until that afternoon when
he showed up at our home in the Malibu Colony. I did not understand
the business of moviemaking, but a big part of the reason we were not
socializing with Hopper was because, at that time, Peter Fonda was in

the midst of a terrible fight with him over money issues connected to the royalties from *Easy Rider* after it had become such an unexpected success and had made so much money.

On the afternoon that Dennis arrived at our house, I was sitting in the living room doing my homework. John was leading Dennis and three other people around to show off the place. I was very surprised to see Dennis in the middle of the afternoon on a school day. His party was made up of two beautiful women and the eighteen-year-old John Paul Getty III, who, I was being told, had had his ear cut off by kidnappers the year before. That was creepy. I tried to ignore them, but they got John stoned and started playing music really loudly. I complained to John that I could not do my homework with such loud music on, but he was excited to have these people to socialize with and said, "They are high on acid and need to hang around for a little while so they can come down."

I packed up my books and went to find a quiet place to work. That's when Dennis noticed me and began following me around the house. He wanted me to sit down and talk with him, but I wouldn't do it, and finally, he turned to the women he'd brought with him and said right in front of me, "Get her in the Jacuzzi. I want to fuck her."

His voice at that moment was the same voice he used some years later when playing a psychopathic drug dealer and pimp in the movie *Blue Velvet*. Because of what would happen that afternoon, I was never able to watch that film, but during the writing of this book, I tried again to sit through it and still couldn't because even now it brings back such vivid, frightening memories. When he used that voice with me, there was no ambiguity to it, and I sensed immediately that if I stuck around, something bad was going to happen to me. I immediately knew I had to get out of the house. Instinct or perhaps the self-defense training Dad had indoctrinated me with kicked in. Though I only had my learner's permit, I grabbed the car keys from the kitchen table and ran upstairs to my room. The two women were following right behind me, and there was no lock on my door, but as I was accustomed to playing on the roof with the neighborhood kids, I climbed out the bathroom window, ran across the roof, shimmied out onto a tree; to the women coming into my room, it was as if I had disappeared. I lowered myself to the ground, ran to the car, and drove away to a girlfriend's house. I stayed with her until Mom and Dad came home. When they got back, I immediately told them what happened, even though I was worried they would get mad at me because I was not supposed to drive the car without a licensed driver accompanying me. They heard me out and had me repeat the story to several family friends, including a man who told me he knew a woman who had been abused by Hopper.

Later that month, Dad told me over dinner with friends that he'd contacted "some people" he knew and had a contract put out on Dennis Hopper to have him kneecapped. He was excited by his Mafia-like solution to the problem and—as was typical of Dad—the story suddenly became a story that was all about him. It wasn't about my frightening experience anymore; now it had become the story of a noble father doing the right thing by his daughter. Beyond that, it was about Dad being a tough guy who knew how to seek out the kind of people who could be hired to permanently damage someone. This, Dad told me, was better than having someone killed; this would be measured revenge. Hopper would be alive, and everyone would know that Larry Hagman's daughter was not to be messed with. He had taken a page right out of our neighbor Mario Puzo's book *The Godfather.*

I have no idea if he actually did get in touch with some leg breakers or if he was telling a totally made-up story to make me feel safe.

Years went by and the story was told again and again, but nothing ever happened to Dennis Hopper. As far as I know, Dad never saw him again, and at some point, Dad began to say that Mom had made him cancel the contract. I suspect he made the whole thing up.

13

A Trip with Dad to Nowhere Land

TEN YEARS AFTER dad took his first acid trip, he asked me to take one with him.

I had just finished my freshman year at San Francisco State. When I came home for the summer, Dad seemed really glad to have me home. Though we were living in Malibu then, it had become our custom to rent our house during the summer to richer celebrities, which gave Dad the money he needed to pay the property taxes and the mortgage. All our personal stuff had to be put away or thrown out so the renters could live in our rooms, and we went off to live somewhere else for a few months.

Sometimes we went camping. One summer, when Dad had some work in the Los Angeles area, we camped out on the Fondas' tennis court; the following summer, I took a trip to Europe on my own. But while Peter Sellers rented our house, Dad, Mom, and my brother, Preston, plus our three cats, two dogs, and one turtle moved into a spare room in the Pando Company offices that Peter Fonda shared with his *Easy Rider* producer Billy Hayward (who in the small world of showbiz was the son of Leland Hayward, who often produced Ganny's shows!). Their office was in a funky bungalow in West Hollywood, where all sorts of people were hanging out and getting high night and day. Dad loved it.

The next summer when I returned from the university, my family was living at Ganny's house in Palm Springs. Like most of her neighbors, Ganny left Palm Springs during the blasting summer heat, so we had the whole neighborhood to ourselves. Because the heat was so stifling, people in the desert tended to stay indoors until it cooled down a bit after 5:00 P.M. Dad and I were stuck in the house and bored when he casually suggested we do LSD together.

The invitation didn't surprise me. It was ten years since he'd taken his first acid trip; I knew that he was all about sharing the tripping experience.

By then, he had stopped trying to get his mother to smoke pot with him and had become very careful not to talk about taking drugs when she was around. But she had no illusions about what he was actually doing or about his attempts to get others to join him. And she didn't mince words when telling him how she felt about it.

"I loathe your going in for this," she'd recently said, "and I have no respect for your desire to have all those you care about share it with you."

If we stayed at her house when she was home, Dad would go out in the orchard to smoke alone and avoid taking hallucinogens. But when Ganny wasn't in the vicinity, he was free to be out in the open with his drug use and to do whatever he wanted.

Though I'd never done hallucinogens with Dad, many of my high school friends had been very casual about dropping acid. I seldom did it. It took too much out of me. It was so intense; I felt I needed days to recover and weeks to feel like myself again. Once I got to college, I avoided pot and did not take LSD at all. I did not know it at the time, but I had a learning disability; school was difficult for me, and taking drugs made schoolwork that much harder to do, so I instinctively avoided it.

I knew firsthand that taking drugs was serious business. Since I was about nine years old, I'd been around people who were tripping. As a kid in Malibu, I was frequently taking care of adults who were too high to take care of themselves. There is something about my character that lends itself to caring for other people, maybe because I was so tuned in to my parents' moods. Dad said many times that he was never hungover after a night of drinking, but I have drawings of him that I did as a teen that show him lying around in a robe looking out of it and the caption "Hungover" scrawled in my handwriting at the bottom of the page. Mom was often in a terrible mood when she woke up. I learned to make her coffee and bring her cigarettes before I went to school, hoping that by doing so she would be in a good mood for the rest of the day. I knew that LSD made people extremely vulnerable. If I took acid with Dad, who would be watching out for me? It was a scary prospect, but I wanted my dad's approval. Though he had always been loving, he'd also been critical; he could be hard on me at times in the belief that he was just trying to help me. For example, during this first year of college, I had missed both my parents a lot but had seldom called home because the first thing I would hear from him was, "Have you lost any weight yet?"

I was not sure I wanted to let my guard down around him. Mom assured me that she would stay straight while we were tripping, and as long as she was with us, I was confident enough that everything would be okay.

Dad kept talking about what great, enlightening experiences he had had on acid. Maybe, I thought, if I tripped with Dad, it would be a way to know him better. Because Dad never liked to talk about his feelings, the way to be close to him was to do things with him—watch the sunset, relax in the Jacuzzi, or sit on the couch and watch TV snuggled up next to him. I did all those things, yet despite these cozy times we spent together, he remained an enigma to me.

Could acid give me that aha! moment of understanding that Dad always talked about? Maybe, by doing acid together, the aha! moment would be about our relationship, and I would at last understand who he was.

So as the desert heat cooled down, we dropped acid holding hands while we watched the sunset. We sat by the pool overlooking the orchard that was filled with lemon, lime, orange, and grapefruit trees. There was a beautiful red-and-purple glow radiating off the mountains that edge Palm Springs. As the sun disappeared behind those mountains and the color faded from the sky, I felt attracted to the blue light in the pool. I took off my dress and slipped into the water that was the same temperature as my skin and gazed down at my pale, naked body, feeling it expand as if my body and the water were one. It was as if I *was* the water filling the pool's entire width and breadth. I felt powerful in that pool; I was completely unafraid. The experience was glorious. I have no idea how long I was in there. At some point, Mom coaxed me out of the water and dried me off and helped me put on one of the robes she made from warm, soft terry cloth that felt so comforting. I was barefoot, and so was Dad, and we tiptoed around the gravel-covered orchard picking grapefruits from the trees. As we peeled them open, each piece of fruit was a marvel, a jewel. We pulled oranges apart too, and each section of pulp was like the fleshy part of my hand just below the thumb, and I wondered if my hand would come apart as easily as the orange did. Dad and I did not talk much. We listened to Handel's *Water Music*, and at some point, we each wandered off in different directions.

I ended up inside the house, moving from room to room, picking things up, and smelling things. The house was filled with the familiar scent that was especially Ganny's, and for a while, I was lost in my memories of playing in her bedroom back in the old days in New York. Those thoughts led me to Ganny's dressing room, which was not at all like the spacious bedroom and open dressing area with its freestanding cheval mirror that had been in her Sutton Place apartment in New York. This was a small, cramped room made to look bigger by the use of mirrors on all four sides. As I entered, I saw images of myself multiplied indefinitely. There were hundreds of me reflecting back at me on the shining surfaces of that small room. It was very disconcerting. I felt a violent urge to bang my fists into the glass over and over, but I managed to get myself out of the room and find my mother.

I told her, "Don't let me go in there again alone." For the rest of the night, she stayed close to me.

I don't think Mom ever felt comfortable tripping, and she understood that I was scared. Dad also seemed to sense my discomfort, and being his jovial self, he found Kleenex boxes and put them on his feet and then shuffled around the house repeating, "I'm Puss in Boots, I'm Puss in Boots," which made all of us laugh uncontrollably. Dad was at his best when he was clowning and making other people happy.

I felt very close to Mom. We were a physical family. We always held each other as we walked down the beach or sat cuddled together when we watched TV. We gave each other butterfly kisses (getting close to the other person's cheek and wiggling your eyelashes to tickle him or her) or Eskimo kisses (rubbing noses), so when I was high, it was natural to hold on to her, and it was comforting to be in her presence. While I sat with her, Dad became absorbed with picking the seeds out of a watermelon, and after a while, having taken stock of how many hours we had been high, Mom made some spaghetti for us, thinking that we might be able to eat and that food would help me come down. We all were familiar with the different stages of trips. Even though each trip was different, there were some similarities to the effects, like a time when it was too overwhelming to eat and a time when your body got hungry and hunger would take you to negative places because of the need for sustenance. By then, it was the middle of the night, and we'd been tripping a long time. Mom got busy making us spaghetti. When the meal was ready, Dad and I sat at the table, fascinated by the intricate lines of pasta, which we played with as much as we ate them.

Being high is a lot of work! Everything you come in contact with becomes an intense exploration that completely takes you over and ultimately becomes exhausting.

Taking LSD with Dad did not, as I hoped it would, occasion any meaningful father-daughter talks. As I've said, Dad was never inclined to have talks of that sort anyway, and the truth is, I was so stoned that I probably would not have remembered any talks if we'd had them. I had to be content with the fact that we were more like playmates than soul mates. For the rest of our lives, we often referred to the trip we took together and spoke of how our outlooks on life had been changed by LSD and of how our experience of real things in our everyday lives, like colors and scents, became more vivid than they had been before taking it.

Even without any kind of interpersonal revelation, that experience in the desert was a milestone that reminded me how intense the drug is and how much time and energy it takes to go on a trip, and it made me understand that Dad, the happy traveler, was comfortable going places where I would never follow him again.

When I tripped with Dad, I still had not told him or my mother about what had happened to me when they left me with Larry Hall. The truth is, I didn't fully understand that awful event until I was twenty-seven and went to a rally held by Take Back the Night, an international group that protests rape and other forms of sexual violence.

At the rally, I learned that a rape can occur even when there isn't vaginal penetration; I learned that being forced to lick a penis under threat of violence is a form of rape. I heard people at the rally say again and again that it was not the fault of the child who was forced to perform such acts. I felt such a sense of unity with the people around me. I felt they would understand me and be a comfort for me, and in turn, I would comfort them. We were not bad; the child in each of us was reaching out to be recognized and made whole. The leaders of the group said it was important to talk about what had happened, to not keep it to yourself. The sharing of the experience made it less power-ful. They allowed that the pain will never go away, but what can be changed is the way the pain causes you to function. Clearly, if more children felt they were safe to talk about what people did to them, they could be cared for, and perpetrators might be confronted or stopped from hurting others.

So one day when we were alone together, I sat my parents down and told them what had happened to me. I tried to present it simply as a story of something that happened a long time ago, something I had put behind me and grown out of. But I started crying as I described what happened in my bedroom while they were away more than two decades earlier. They just looked away and didn't say anything. Nothing.

Not a word. The silence seemed to last forever. It was obvious that Dad had no idea about how to respond and did not know what to say. I wanted them to comfort me as the kindly strangers did at the rally. I wanted them to say they were so sorry such a terrible thing had happened to me, as Larry Hall had done. I wanted them to hug me. I wanted them to tell me what I had learned at the rally: I wanted them to say, "It was not your fault."

But Dad mumbled something that I could not hear between my sobs, and he went into the other room. What I'd told them was just too tough for him. There was no way he could turn what I'd told him into a funny story and make us laugh the way he usually would when anything was said that was uncomfortable for him. Mom just shook her head. She did not say a word, and she did not reach out to me. I felt as alone as I had when the incident occurred. I was weak from crying.

After Dad died, it struck me that the fact that he'd failed to comfort me at a time when I so sorely needed comforting might be something for which, in his final moments, he might have asked me to forgive him for. But I'm pretty sure he had put the whole matter out of his thoughts long before, not because he was uncaring but because he had been so saddened by what I had told him that he could never bear to think of it again.

In those last precious hours before he lost consciousness, the connection we shared was a time of healing for us both. So I hope he wasn't thinking of it. I wouldn't want him to be feeling that he'd failed me in any way—big or small—as he slipped away from this world.

14

Malibu

I N 1966, DAD HAD BOUGHT us a shabby beach house in Malibu
Colony. Back in 1927, carpenters from one of the movie studios
had built the house that became our new home as a temporary weekend rental for movie stars. The house evolved over the years and had
been expanded in a kind of do-it-yourself way and without plans. But
the fairly dismal quality of the construction did not matter to my parents; this house was right on the beach, and Mom was overjoyed that
she was finally the owner of her own home. Buying this house was an
amazing feat because of Dad's habit of spending any cash he earned
right away. It was the physical manifestation of the fact that he'd really
had some financial success as an actor. He very rightly kept saying that
he really couldn't afford it, but Mom found ways of making money so
that we could hold on to our beautiful ocean view.

After my experience with the kids in my neighborhood in Santa
Monica, I became a bit of a loner when we moved to Malibu. I played

with Peter Fonda's kids when they stayed with us, but they were quite a bit younger than I was. I also made friends with the girls next door, who were a bit older, but many of the kids in the Colony teased me. They said we were weird because everyone who came to our house wore robes and bathed nude. My dad was different, and these kids couldn't understand the flag parades down the beach and all the strange outfits Dad wore to the grocery store. I spent a lot of my time at home, cooking with my mom and painting, and I took long walks. In those days, dogs roamed free. I love animals and made friends with all the dogs on the beach. I brought treats with me, and sometimes I walked the length of the Colony and kept going way up into the Malibu hills where Pepperdine University now stands, with a pack of ten or twelve dogs around me. I felt safe and free.

We were all friends with the Hormel family, famed for their sausage and lunch meats. Dad had played Prince Charming to their widowed matriarch. The Hormels had a whole bunch of kids. We always had fun together when they came to their own little cottage on the north end of the beach. We played with a giant silk army/navy surplus parachute that the tall men would make billow above all the children, and their big family made a great team for playing Frisbee.

There were very few girls in our neighborhood of my age, so I was very excited when a new girl came to live down the beach from me one summer. She was from back east and had a very sweet and gentle manner. Before Kate arrived, everyone on the beach was so excited that her family had rented a house for the summer because she was Richard Burton's daughter, and she was summering with her father and his then wife, Elizabeth Taylor. Even as a kid, I knew these were especially famous people, having stared up at their faces painted ten feet tall on the billboard advertising their film *Cleopatra* when I was a was living in New York. For months, this glamorous couple had graced our neighborhood. I remembered them as the most beautiful people ever imaginable.

But when I actually got to know Kate, her famous father and stepmother and their notorious love affair were not what interested me. Kate was the best thing that happened on the beach that summer. I was drawn to how solid she was, how she seemed to be a girl who'd had the kind of meticulous and careful upbringing my parents, with their freewheeling lifestyle, had not given me. Her mother, Sybil Burton, was British and had been an actress, though she had given up acting soon after she married to focus on her husband and their children. After their very public and messy divorce, she continued to be a devoted mother while at the same time becoming the queen of New York nightlife. At the height of the disco era, she created one of the hippest discotheques in the city, called Arthur, where all the stars went to drink and dance.

Though her mother was not with her in Malibu, I took note of how often Kate said things like, "I have to rinse my hair after being in the ocean; my mom says it is not good to have salt water in your hair all day," or "I can't play right now; Mom says I have to read several books before I go home," or "I shouldn't eat chocolate because it's bad for my complexion."

I did not have anyone giving me instructions like this. I was something of a wild child. I paid attention to everything about her: Kate did not wear flashy clothes, but there was something very cool about the way she put things together. The quality of her outfits and the way she looked fascinated me. As we became better friends, she told me she had a small role in one of her dad's movies, *Anne of the Thousand Days*. It was the story of Henry VIII and Anne Boleyn, and Kate had a part as a servant girl. She was long gone from Malibu by the time I saw her in that film. I got my parents to take me to the theater to see it a couple of times, and I've never forgotten how classy she was.

Over the years, I have watched her consistent success as an actress while at the same time raising her children. I was so happy to see that she got rave reviews in important plays like *Hedda Gabler* and *The Cherry Orchard*. She also did a lot of noteworthy work on TV in *Grey's Anatomy* and later as the vice president in *Scandal*. I am sure that she must still be the wonderful person I knew that summer.

Because Kate had gotten to work with her dad, I started asking my dad if I could work with him. He knew how important it was to me, and he made sure I appeared in a movie with him the very next year. It was a movie that Peter Fonda directed and starred in, and it was called *The Hired Hand*. The film was being shot in New Mexico; Dad played a bearded sheriff, and one day, I came on the set to watch him work. As soon as I arrived, the costume lady smiled at me, took my hand, and led me over to a big truckful of Western costumes. Half an hour later, I had been transformed into a Western girl from the late 1800s. I did not have a speaking part; I was just sitting on a barrel as my dad's character walked by, but it was still a thrill to be in the movie. The film was called a hippie Western by reviewers, but it was still a special experience, and to this day, I cherish the photos of the two of us together, looking happy and full of love for each other in our Western costumes.

After *I Dream of Jeannie* wasn't renewed, Dad's income became more unpredictable again. That is why we started to rent our beach home out. We didn't need to move out permanently because renting it out for just a few months each summer, when the Colony became filled with what we called "summer people," paid enough to cover our basic expenses for the whole year while we took off to live in a tent some-where. Summer also happened to be the time of year when TV pro-duction was on hiatus, so Dad would not be working on a pilot or TV series. Sometimes I wished we could enjoy the beach when school was out, and the annual ritual of packing up all my private things and having someone else sleep in my room altered the way I felt about home. It gave me the belief, early on, that home was where my family was rather than it being whatever structure we lived in. There were some years when we did not leave the LA area while the house was rented, and I would find a way to get to the beach so I could walk by the house and look up at it longingly. Mom was always making im-provements to the beach cottage, and my room eventually had a big window and French doors that opened onto an oceanfront balcony through which the sounds of the waves lulled me to sleep every night. It was a beautiful room, and I appreciated it all the more because I had to leave for a few months every year. As summer approached, I be-came anxious because I never knew where we would live till we were in the car and on our way. In preparation for the renters, Mom would remodel the house, doing a lot of the hard physical work herself with her own hands. She loved building homes even more than she liked making clothes.

Mom poured the prodigious energy that she had previously focused on being a dress designer into rebuilding our Malibu house. Often, money was tight for making the home improvements she envisioned, so she would tear down walls with her own hands and build them up again as she saw fit. Dad bought her power tools as birthday and Christmas presents. I liked working with her to rebuild and redeco-rate. While Preston and Dad were out hunting, Mom and I bonded over building things. We would go to the lumberyard together, where everyone knew her, and she would ask lots of questions about how to put a specific thing together. She knew how to select the straightest boards and just the right balance of ingredients to make grout for tile so it would withstand bad weather.

She had transformed every place we had ever lived in, from pulling out the drawer in hotel rooms to turn it into a crib for me, to knocking down walls in our New York apartment, to building my beloved room in Malibu.

Mom liked the feeling of exhaustion she felt at the end of a hard physical workday. Dad proudly spoke of how she had remodeled our apartment back in New York City by carrying each bucket of plaster down the five flights of stairs to discreetly deposit the debris into public waste bins so no one would know she was tearing down walls.

Our house in Malibu became her passion, and using the excuse that it needed to be spruced up for the renter, she made it more beautiful year by year. Slowly, she changed everything about it, and in 1982 she tore the whole place down and built a new stunning home of her own design on the site.

But there was one thing she didn't tear down, and that was her masterpiece, the Jacuzzi. The Jacuzzi was the heart of our home; it was literally and figuratively in the center of it, and the new house was built around it. We had had it since we'd moved to Malibu in the *I Dream of Jeannie* days.

Mom had heard about the Jacuzzi brothers, engineers who had found a way to use the healing power of hot water to care for their family members with arthritis. They had invented a hydrotherapy pump that mixed air and water to massage your body while you were in a hot tub. Mom was intrigued, but she wanted to incorporate the spa into our home as if it were bubbling out of a grotto. Somehow she got in touch with the Jacuzzi brothers and told them about our family's love of natural hot springs. She said she did not want to buy a plastic box fitted with Jacuzzi pumps; she wanted to build an environment that had the flowing, gently curved lines of waterworn rocks found in nature, and she wanted to place the pumps to their best advantage. They worked with her and made the pumps available for her custom use. She decided that the heads would be placed at different heights and that the tub would be so deep in places that you could stand up and still be submerged in water as more water spurted from the Jacuzzi heads.

She then found a company that had a device that shot concrete out of a hose so you could attach it to a metal armature and create free-flowing shapes. Ultimately, what she created was a magical, organically shaped, black-bottomed pool that had the sensual curves of a Henry Moore sculpture. As far as I know, no one else ever made anything like it. We all went into the Jacuzzi before going off for the day and then again before bed each night. We all loved it, and bathing together became central to our lives.

Another regular part of life with the industrious women in my family was that we were always making things that Dad would then use to stage his happenings. One month, we sewed a hundred flags, no two of which were alike, for Dad to pass out to everyone willing to carry one when he held his flag parades on the beach every Sunday at sunset. What that meant was that each Sunday, as the afternoon light began to fade, our house would empty out, and we would all walk down the beach with armloads of tall flagpoles topped with multicolored flags. These flags were very colorful, and some had antiwar slogans or civil rights slogans written on them. I remember one proclaiming the Age of Aquarius, but mostly they were just props to get people to have fun. Dad would play the flute and encourage people to come out of their houses and join us. There was no set meaning or purpose for these parades, though they did have a pattern. Once he had assembled a good number of people, maybe twenty or more, we would all walk down the beach with our flags flowing overhead, with Dad at the helm, making music and turning himself into a beach-bound Pied Piper. At the end of the Colony's private beach, he would get everyone to temporarily plant their flags and join hands, and then he would instruct them all in "gong bong." I have no idea where he got the idea, but it became a tradition; we would hold hands and take ten very deep, loud breaths together as Dad counted them down; then, on the tenth breath, which he tried to coordinate with the sun tipping over the horizon, every one of us—now completely hyperventilating—was to yell out, "Gong bong!" Then we stumbled around giggling until we could find our balance again and walk home happy, collecting the flags as we went.

Another tradition Dad had was silent Sundays. For this, he created an alter ego he called Hagmananda Listens. As I sat down to write about this, I wanted to find a description of it in Dad's own words. First, I picked up his autobiography, but neither Hagmananda nor silent Sundays were listed in the index, so I went to the Internet. Hurray for the Internet! I did a search for "Hagmananda Listens" and found an interview in which Dad described how he'd had a throat infection and the doctor recommended he stop talking for a while. He told the interviewer that "not talking was gloriously therapeutic," and he also told her that I was not thrilled with him after his first silent day. It seems I had written him a note that read, "As you know, I love you very much, but yesterday you were a big s——."

What he did not tell the interviewer was how demanding he had been that day. When he was filming a TV series, he worked long hours during the week, and it was the household policy that when he was home on the weekends, we were to do *everything* we could to make him happy and help him rest for the week to come. We made him any meal he wanted or just simply fetched things for him so he did not have to get up; he called us "gofers," which meant, "You go for this and go for that." Being silent did not mean that Dad was any less demanding; instead of saying go fetch something or sweetly asking us to make him one of his favorite tuna melt sandwiches, he did elaborate pantomimes so that we had to stop what we were doing and spend a half an hour playing charades with him so that one of us could finally decipher just exactly what he wanted. He found these interactions so entertaining that he came up with more things he needed and more and more elaborate menus for us to serve him; my playful father commanded our total attention and he did all he could to make the game last longer. On one such occasion, he wanted to have caviar on little triangular pieces of thin white toast topped with sour cream and decoratively sprinkled with chopped egg and red onion, served on his grandmother's gold-rimmed china from storage. If I did not get something right, he made a big fuss and gestured that I had to start from the beginning again. When I became frustrated, he laughed at me. As usual, there was no sense in talking to him if you were upset about something; he would just tune you out by whistling, which was one of the nonverbal ways he communicated even on his silent days.

After we moved to Malibu, we had the help of our live-in maid, Rosa, to clean up after us, the women of the household—Mom and I—continued to do all the cooking aided by my aunts who had moved close by and spent every weekend with us. Our home was always filled with delicious smells and bustling with activity as we made things—cooking, sewing, painting, and hammering. Mom would say the Swedish answer to depression or boredom was to keep busy, and Dad knew that a productive wife was a happy wife. He would order up some wild thing that caught his fancy—a satin cape, or a pirate outfit, or a box to hold his flutes—and Mom would whip out her sewing machine or her toolbox and make it before the day was over. If it was something she did not know how to do, the aunts and I would figure it out. In addition, I painted murals for him, and one of my aunts made a special stand to keep extra-large books at chest height for comfortable browsing and opened to a certain page.

All the ladies would decorate the table for special dinners with themes like the Indian raj dinner. As we cooked, Dad would tell the story of how the British raj would have elaborate dinners with handsomely dressed serving boys standing at the back of everyone's chair ready to present another exotic condiment. We did our best to re-create the luxury of the image he conjured for us. When the curry was presented on the table, it was covered in Indian cloth with matching napkins, incense, Indian candleholders, and exotic flowers. There were also twelve bowls of condiments: chutneys and chopped egg, peanuts, banana, raisins, onion, chilies, parsley, cucumber, grated orange rind, coconut, and candied ginger.

We had people over for dinner several nights a week. Dad held court in a little open bar between the Jacuzzi and the dining hall that was mainly stocked with lots of inexpensive champagne, wine, and beer. The huge dining hall had a table that sat twelve comfortably. After dessert, we would dance in front of a nine-by-twelve-foot stained glass window depicting wild, giant, psychedelic flowers, mushrooms, and butterflies that my aunt Lillimor had made according to my dad's specification. It was lit from behind at night. To enhance the dance palace atmosphere, and in keeping with the disco craze of the 1970s, Dad had someone put up a rotating mirrored ballroom ball with a spotlight that sent white sparkles whirling around the room.

Last I heard, Sting, who bought the house from us, has kept this room just as it was when we lived in the house. I hope people are still dancing there after dinner.

My personal favorite dance partners were Joel Grey and his daughter, Jennifer. They lived just two doors away. We loved to dance to Harry Nilsson's song "Coconut": "Put the lime in the coconut, then you'll feel better . . ." I haven't seen Jenny in years, but I had breakfast with Joel not long ago, and we talked about art and family and love. Sitting with him, I felt comfortable in the way that one only feels with someone after having shared a piece of one's true self. The lime in the coconut is like the password that brings us back to those fun evenings spent singing and dancing for no special occasion and only for the grateful celebration of the joy of life.

My parents were great hosts. The combination of my father as magician/master of ceremonies and my industrious mother, who did everything she could to create the exotic environment he dreamed up, made our home a truly transformative place. People would arrive with all their emotional baggage, and bit by bit, they would put it down as they went for walks on the beach or played Frisbee and took a few tokes on a joint and drank some champagne. Time melted away.

There was lots of pot and wine, and there was lots of food too. We were always preparing delicious things, and I frequently ran barefoot to the nearby grocery store to buy more food. People loved coming to our house. You could see them unwinding after spending an hour or two in our home. Everyone would have a long soak in the Jacuzzi, and after a relatively short time, those who had entered our home had changed completely from the harried, encumbered people they had been to happier versions of themselves. Now they were calm and free of inhibitions. Almost everyone who ever walked through our door was someone I saw wet and naked before they left our house.

When our guests came out of the Jacuzzi, their nude bodies were kept comfortable and warm by the beautiful terry cloth robes my mother and aunts made. Mom had used her clothing designer skills to make robes in many different sizes and colors with decorative gold-embroidered trim. Dad called them monks' robes, but the trim made them look more regal than religious. Mom hunted for these special trims in all the fabric stores near the clothing factories in downtown LA, and I went with her just as I had when I was a child.

These robes had hoods like monk's robes, and they were wide and flowing so everyone could maintain their newly felt sense of freedom; at the same time, these robes were a uniform that allowed any group of disparate people to merge into one.

Even now, when I run into my friends from high school, they tell me—forty years later—that the best and wildest parties they ever went to were at my house with my parents.

There is a photograph that was published in *Vogue* of me entering naked into the Jacuzzi with my parents and my brother, Preston, in the tub, all of them looking up at me; Dad, who always knew where the camera was, looked somewhat hazily at the photographer, but it really wouldn't have been any different if the photographer were not there at all. This picture was a slice of our everyday life. The caption next to the picture was a quote from my dad: "The family that bathes together stays together." That idea is radical even today. At that time, it had never occurred to me that there was anything the least bit unusual about our family being naked together. The nakedness was part of the era, but it was also part of how our family interacted; it was natural.

Dad was not concerned with moral issues like whether nudity was appropriate. He worried about big issues like nuclear holocaust and natural disasters. He always had backpacks filled with shoes and eye-glasses, first aid kits, and water filters. This was true from my early childhood and continued until the day he died. In Malibu, we had a big space under the stairs in our house where he stashed away twenty-gallon tubs of dried food, beans, rice, pasta, as well as space blankets, cash, and a high-frequency radio. He loved living by the beach but talked frequently about his fear of tsunamis. BB the nurse put to-gether the emergency kits that were kept by the front door because he was always talking about the need to be prepared for earthquakes and for the tsunami that he was certain would come from Japan one day.

A little more than a year before Dad died, I got a call from him. He was in a Paris airport; it was at 5:00 A.M. my time. I am an early riser, but not that early, and I was barely awake when I answered the phone. He sounded very worried and asked, "Have you heard about the tsunami? Are you okay? Are the kids safe? Is Noel okay?"

Noel, my brother's daughter and the firstborn of the five Blondies, was staying in Dad's apartment. I shook my head and asked what he was talking about. He said there had been an earthquake in Japan that was going to send a tsunami to the coast of California. "Do you have enough gas in your car," he wanted to know, "so you can get to high ground?"

"Now do exactly what I tell you to do," he continued. "Turn on the news and take a look at what is happening, then get gas in your car. Next, go straight to my condo and check on Noel. I can't reach her by phone, and the condo is right over the ocean. I won't board my next flight till I hear back from you when I know that you're all safe. Do you have that?"

"Yes, Dad, okay. I've got it!"

I jumped out of bed and went on the Internet, where I saw terrifying images of the giant wave washing away an entire town in Japan. I did not linger. I followed Dad's orders exactly as I had been trained to do on our hunting trips when I was a child. I checked on my kids. I jumped in my car. I got gas and went straight to his condo. After rushing like mad, it felt surreal to find myself looking out the windows of the elevator at a beautiful sunrise and the ocean spread out below me as calm as glass. I stepped out of the elevator, and I rang the doorbell. There was no answer. I rang again to report news of a coming disaster that there was no evidence of . . . Still Noel did not answer. I was not sure what I should do. Dad said he would not get on his next flight until I called him back with the report that everyone was safe, so I went to the back entrance of the condo. I used my key and went in, saying hello in a loud voice, but though Noel's stuff was lying all around the place, no one answered my calls. Before turning to leave, I thought I would make one last attempt to do what I was told to do. I knocked on the bedroom door. At least then I could tell Dad I did everything I could to check on his eldest granddaughter. Just as I was turning to go, Noel came out of the bedroom wrapped in a sheet. She looked at me like I was crazy. I told her that Grandpa wanted to make sure she was safe because there was a tsunami coming from Japan. She said something like, "You have got to be kidding," and then we both looked out of the giant wraparound floor-to-ceiling windows at a picture-perfect day. With embarrassment, I turned and left. As soon as I got into my car, I called Dad, telling him that there did not appear to be any danger. He had been waiting to hear from me, and now he quickly proceeded to board his flight.

That beautiful sunny day continued with unusually low surf. But after years of Dad's contemplating this precise disaster, I decided to keep my daughter at home instead of letting her go to her high school, which was only four blocks from the beach. I wanted to be absolutely sure there was no danger because for years and years, Dad had been saying the "big wave was coming."

Though we were safe that day, Dad took the Fukushima disaster as a sign that the next big one might really hit his Santa Monica penthouse. When he returned from his trip, he bought an electric bike to use as a getaway vehicle in case the next tsunami were to pose a threat to his his life. The bike was like an off-road vehicle with studded tires and big panniers to hold all his emergency gear. He was eighty-one years old then, but he was ready to be a road warrior.

Dad in the backyard learning how to handle a gun with his father, Ben Hagman, and half brother, Gary, in Weatherford, Texas

Mom and Dad camping in the Hamptons when I was a baby

One of the many photos taken on the bed that day. (Don Loomis)

Age 3 with Mom and Dad. Dad wears his favorite beaver coat and Mom is in clothes she made for herself.

Dad sitting and reading in the screened-in front porch Mom invented and made so that camping would be more comfortable

Camping near a glacier
stream in Canada

The day I became a Girl Scout. This was
also the day before I came home from
school to find a bunch of teenage boys
in my bedroom. (Larry Hall)

Me (age 15) and Dad in
front of the mural I painted
on our garage door

Dad's birthday at
home in Malibu

Mom and Dad

Dad in one of his favorite outfits, proudly sitting in his custom-made van. (Nancy Ellison/Polaris)

Ganny hired her favorite photographer to take my head shots when I was a young actress auditioning in Hollywood. They were beautiful photos but they looked more vintage than of a girl in the 1980s who worked at the Comedy Store. (Jo Bill Hiedger)

Ganny and me

Mom and me dressed up to go to the Santa Fe Opera

Dad with me, Ganny, and Mom at my first Los Angeles art opening. (Bill Nation)

Dad visits Santa Fe and stages this photo as a way of saying he was sorry. (Daniel Masler)

Dad with shiny red lizard on his shoulder at Pike Place Market, Seattle

Photos of Dad dressed as a cowboy good guy in white hat and suit riding down the center of Wilshire Boulevard on the way to the auction at Julien's in Beverly Hills were featured in newspapers around the world. (Darren Julien and Martin Nolan)

Having lunch with Mom and Dad after her Alzheimer's had set in

A typical weekend in Malibu

15

Finding Work, *Dallas*, and Fame

During the years between *I Dream of Jeannie* and *Dallas*, we lived in high hippie mode following Dad's lead. On top of taking hallucinogens regularly, he experimented with Eastern mysticism, vegetarianism, pacifism, and lots of other isms. These activities superseded his ambition to be the best and most famous actor on television. In those days, his interests were guided by ideological slogans: Stop the War, Give Peace a Chance, and Be Here Now.

Dad wanted to align his work life with his beliefs, so he refused any work that portrayed violence, which limited the parts he went after. Though Dad, as a teenager living with his father in Texas, had taken to owning guns and enjoying the local hunting culture, he had totally turned away from those pastimes and interests. Instead, he immersed himself in the Malibu lifestyle. His priorities became the joy of being on the beach and playing Frisbee at the edge of the surf. He became so committed to this new way of life and thinking that he avoided guns completely and wouldn't even let my brother have a toy gun or war toys of any kind. But like many hippie parents who took this stance, Dad found that little boys, like my brother, will invariably take a stick and turn it into a sword or gun.

When Preston hit adolescence, Dad started to pay more attention to what his son was interested in; he realized that he was out of touch with his boy. So he changed his stance and used guns and the hunting culture as a way to reach out to Preston. This was history repeating itself; Dad was using the same tactics that his dad had used to get close to him when he'd returned to Texas after being separated from his father since early childhood. Once they found an activity to bond over, Dad and Preston became much closer. For the rest of their lives together, the two of them went hunting several times a year, and when Dad died, as mementos of their time together, my brother became the recipient of Dad's collection of guns.

Adolescence is not an easy time for anyone and I had was struggling both academically and socially. I was very unhappy in public school. My learning disability caused me to be in some remedial classes and, as they had when I was much younger, kids teased me for being a misfit. I wanted desperately to find some adult guidance. I felt that the year I started high school would be a chance to make a big change in my life. So I convinced my parents to send me to a new alternative school that was just being started in Santa Monica. Sadly for me, the new school, though based on well-meaning hippie values, was very disorganized; it was not the supportive learning environment I craved. With my parents' consent, I dropped out of that school during the last half of ninth grade to do an independent study program that the headmaster set up for me. My assignment was to help one of the teachers collect data for her advanced degree in education. She had me interview middle school–aged kids in Watts about their school experiences. Though I only did a few interviews, no one could have found a better course of study to convince a young person about the importance of a good education. I learned how to articulate what kind of school I was looking for, and Mom contacted a learning specialist who found the place that would be a perfect fit for me, but it was a long drive away from Malibu, in the San Fernando Valley.

Oakwood High School was an alternative school that had a mission to respect students by fostering creativity and establishing a conscious-ness of community. It was much like the Woodstock Country School that Dad had attended and loved. My first year there, I blossomed. I found teachers there who really understood who I was and challenged me. The other students were like me: curious about the world and eager to learn from caring adult mentors. I loved the school and really wanted to finish high school there, but over the summer, Dad told me he could not afford the tuition. He said he was broke again. He reminded me that he was not getting enough work to pay the bills because many of the roles he was offered would require him to play murderous characters who killed people and thus promoted gun violence.

At my school, students were encouraged to question authority. So I confronted Dad about his mode of protest.

I asked if he had let anyone in the media know about the stance he had taken on gun violence and why he was not accepting violent roles. When he told me he'd never made a public statement about it, I replied that his protest did not make sense to me since no one but his family knew why he was not working. This was a new kind of discussion for us to be having. I remember it as clear as day, and I wrote in my diary about it. I was really tough on him. I said, "If you want to say something that would make the world a better place, I want to do it with you, but what you are doing now is asking me to sacrifice the best school experience I have ever had for nothing. Nobody knows why you're turning down so many of the jobs you're offered. You are not changing anything."

Money was such a difficult issue in our family. Even as a child, I always felt guilty about being supported by my parents, because as long as I could remember, there had been talk about how hard up we were. I wanted to do everything I could to ease their burden, and I stayed busy doing anything that made money, like giving art lessons and painting murals and cooking for neighbors. I did not understand why our financial situation was so precarious. It is only now, after Dad died, that I have tried to piece together what was really going on. I have had long conversations with friends of the family about my parents' repeated portrayals of money troubles. All during the time we were "broke," *Jeannie* was on the air in reruns. No one could understand why Dad was not getting a piece of that action. The reason, as Dad told it, was that Ronald Reagan had messed things up for actors. He had been the head of the Screen Actors Guild six years before *Jeannie* went on the air. Dad said Reagan had not fought for actors to get a fair share of the profits from residuals. He said Reagan did not believe the public wanted to see a show more than twice, so after a show was aired a few times, all the money went to the producers. I cannot vouch for the veracity of this story, but I heard it from my father often. Still, it's hard to see why jobs were in such short supply since there were plenty of shows that did not call for gun violence. In fact, Dad was working regularly throughout the '70s. There was *The Good Life* in '71, though it was canceled midseason, and then he was in *Here We Go Again*, which was also canceled early. He also did guest appearances on other shows.

One of the best gigs he got during the '70s was when he got a job in London working with Lauren Bacall in a TV version of the Broadway show *Applause*. As usual, we all went on location with him. This was the first time my brother and I got to go to England, the place where our parents met and were married. We stayed at the home of one of Dad's oldest friends, the writer Robert Carrington. Bob had a big run-down apartment just off Kensington High Street that had not been cared for in decades. I loved it because I had my own garret in the domed turret of the old building just like the one the protagonist has in *The Little Princess*, which was one of my favorite childhood stories. It was magical. Each day I would go to the gated public garden in the square just outside the flat and pick violets that I'd arrange in a glass bottle and keep beside my cot. While we were in England, we toured around the British Isles and had real hands-on encounters with history. We did things kids cannot do anymore. These days, ancient historic monuments are recognized as delicate and irreplaceable, but when my brother and I were in England, we straddled medieval sarcophagi in Westminster Abbey and made rubbings of their brass plaques by laying a sheet of paper on them and tracing over the plaques' engravings. This was so much fun, but by the mid-'70s, making brass rubbings at the abbey was no longer allowed. At Stonehenge, we climbed over and around the monolithic stones that had been knocked to the ground, while Dad recounted fascinating myths and legends about the people said to have built them.

But being pulled out of school in my teens had challenges that I had not had to face when I was in grade school. For example, in 1973, we spent quite a lot of time in Chile, where Dad did a movie with Trini Lopez called *Antonio;* it was in the same year that we went to London, where he played in the Comden and Green musical *Applause.* I was trying to teach myself geometry, and once a week, I had to take several trains on the London Underground to get to my math tutor. Riding urban public transport was a culture shock for a sheltered girl who had lived mostly in Malibu, and I did not have the tools to cope with all the strange people who confronted me in the city. When I got back home to my high school, I was well behind my classmates academically.

The comments that accompanied my grades from my first year at Oak-wood paint the picture of a girl who did not know the material and was always tired in class. I was sent to the principal because my English teachers thought I was on drugs. When confronted with this accusation, I told the head of school that I was up late several nights a week because we had so many people coming over to our house and I drank wine with the grown-ups at dinner almost every night.

After my interview with the headmaster, the school contacted my parents and recommended we all go to family counseling, but my dad didn't really want to go. I finally convinced him to try it, and all four of us met with a female therapist. In that session, I talked about how hard it was to study at home with all the entertaining they were doing and how much I worried about our financial situation. The therapist was very supportive and encouraged me to express my feelings, but I think I was the only one in the family who liked the session. Both Mom and Preston said very little. When it was Dad's turn to talk, he let me know just how pissed off he was by what I had said, and he made it perfectly clear that he did not want to have anyone criticize his behavior, especially not his daughter. "Darling daughter, you can say anything you want to say because it's water off a duck's back to me. Nothing you say will change the way I feel about you nor the way I conduct my life. I am number one, and I am always going to take care of number one first, and you should do the same for yourself."

I had often heard Dad say, "You have to look out for number one," meaning yourself, but this time, the statement, spoken through clenched teeth in front of the whole family and the therapist, frightened me. I was worried that I would never have my father's affection and approval again, and his words shut me up very effectively for a long, long time.

We never went to the follow-up visit the therapist suggested, but I thought a lot about what Dad had said, and I came to the conclusion that for me, taking care of number one would mean staying at my school. After that session, I had identified a clear goal for myself, and I was determined to continue at Oakwood. In order to do this, I began to search for any way possible to make money, even though I was only fifteen years old.

I looked to my mother for inspiration because she had always found unorthodox ways to earn enough cash to pay our mortgage and other bills. Now it was my turn to find ways to make enough that I could stay at the private high school I loved.

My parents' friends up and down the beach knew what a good cook I was; they had been coming over for dinner and eating my food for years. If Mom was too tired to cook for everybody, I made dinner. However chaotic our home was, it was well known that there was always good food in our house and that dinner would be on the table sometime after sunset. For example, Jane Fonda and Roger Vadim's daughter, Vanessa, was just a toddler when she learned to walk into our house and open the fridge to find something to eat. Jerry Brown was another friend who dropped in often. He was California's secretary of state at the time and was dating Linda Ronstadt, who lived down the beach. She was busy making music, so he would often show up at our house at dinnertime. Dad was always happy to invite him in for a meal, but once, I turned him away before Dad saw him. It was an evening when I was struggling with schoolwork, and I knew if we had company that I would have to stop what I was doing to cook up something especially good. I saw Jerry walking up the steps to our house from the beach, so I quickly got up from the kitchen table where I was working and stopped him at the top of the stairs. I handed him a can of Progresso soup and a can opener and told him that dinner was not happening that night.

Whenever Dad threw a wrap party for a show he was in, I always did a lot of the cooking, sometimes for as many as two hundred people. Mealtime was always important in my family. Wherever we lived, our home glowed with comfort, and ever since we had moved to Malibu, my mother made sure that we prepared the most welcoming homecoming for Dad every night. We would have the fire lit, there would always be flowers and candles on the beautifully set table, and dinner would be cooked and ready the moment he walked in the door so I thought maybe I could cook for people to make money.

I was on the lookout for any way to implement my plan to make enough money to stay in my private high school, and as luck would have it, my friend Jonine offered to let me help her with a job her father gave her. During spring break, she had wanted to keep busy and asked her father, Cal Bernstein, if she could work at his production company, Dove Films. She envisioned going to his office and answering phones, but the only job he had available at that time was for a caterer to feed the cast and crew of a commercial shoot he was doing at a circus. This might sound like an ambitious undertaking for a fifteen-year-old girl, but Cal had a lot of faith in his daughter; he was confident that she could do it. Cal was what we would now call a "foodie": he wrote a restaurant guide and shared his love of good food with his daughter. From the beginning of my friendship with Jonine, her very warm and supportive parents had included me at family dinners that took place at unusual and interesting restaurants all over LA. They took me out for my first sushi meal, and over my first bite of raw fish, we talked about the possibility of Jonine and I working together to cook for the filming at the circus. Jonine's mom came up with some suggestions that would lighten our load on that first job, like getting already poached salmon. With great optimism, we started a catering business. I was a few months older than Jonine and had just gotten my license, but for the first few months after passing the driver's test, teen drivers are not allowed to drive other minors who are not family members, so her mother drove us around on our first jobs. Between Jonine's family connections and mine, we got a lot of work. In fact, our business became so successful that we were reviewed in *The New York Times*.

Later that same year, *The Times*'s renowned food critic Craig Claiborne included some of our recipes in his new book *Craig Claiborne's Favorites* along with an article about spending a day with Jonine and me. On that day he brought the great French chef Jacques Pépin; they joked that they were there to make sure the teenagers were really cooking without any adult help. We were very nervous, but both men were amazingly charming and complimentary. They followed us as we walked across the sand to serve lunch for our neighbor Burgess Meredith and his guests and Mr. Claiborne dubbed us "the barefoot contessas of Malibu." I remember standing at the buffet table, helping to serve people and explaining what was in the food. At the time, most catering was standard American fare or strictly French food à la Julia Child, but our menus included food from all over Europe. The items we served that day included a cheese appetizer using a Swiss raclette machine that melted the cheese with dramatic presentation; this was followed by French lemon chicken, Greek spanakopita, a vegetarian dish that Jonine and I made up, and a Swedish princess torte for dessert. Burgess entertained frequently, and his parties attracted guests from all over the country and well beyond the entertainment world. I was just cutting into a new platter of food when I looked up to greet the next guest. I found myself looking at a man's belt buckle instead of his face. The man was Wilt Chamberlain, the great seven-foot-one basketball player.

By cooking, I made enough money to pay for the first semester of eleventh grade. When Dad saw what I was able to do and how much I cared about staying in Oakwood, his attitude about paying for the school changed. He came up with the money to pay my tuition for the rest of high school even though he was telling everyone that he was broke.

From a teenager's perspective, it appeared that we were living this wonderful carefree life on the beach, but the way Dad kept speaking about our financial situation made all of us feel a great deal of instability.

Mom reacted by trying to make everything she could with her own hands, from designing and building Jacuzzis for our neighbors, like producer Jerry Hillman, to making our clothes and doing house repairs herself. Other than renting the house out every summer, there never seemed to be a plan or budget.

According to Dad, we only had enough cash to live month to month, and it made me anxious. By my junior year in high school, the constant worry about money changed the carefree beach lifestyle. Mom and Dad were yelling at each other. Mom got fed up with all the people coming over uninvited. She put up a hand-painted sign on the gate outside our house that read, "If you have not been invited, don't even think of ringing the bell." Preston was withdrawn, and when I went off to college, I was barely able to make enough to stay in school. Dad became so desperate to change the family dynamic that at one point he borrowed $20,000 and then blew half of it on a family skiing trip because he figured we had to go somewhere to lift our spirits.

Dad really did believe that if he were in a happier state of mind with all his loved ones around him that things would get better. He was right, because it was on that trip that he and Mom looked at two scripts for TV pilots in which he had been offered roles; one of those scripts was *Dallas*.

The role of J. R. Ewing was perfect for Dad; it took him back to his roots, to his teenage years in Weatherford, Texas, with his father, Ben, who was bigger than life in a Texas macho kind of way. To the degree that Dad identified as any one thing, it was as a Texan. He knew the vernacular, the swagger; he knew how to be one of the good old boys.

Dad repeatedly said that his inspiration for the character of J. R. Ewing was a Texan named Jess Hall. The Halls were the richest family in Weatherford, and Dad's father had been Jess's lawyer. While Ben wanted to teach young Larry what it meant to work hard, he asked Jess Hall to give him a job making oil-drilling equipment. The working conditions were terrible; Dad found himself laboring in a tin shack where the temperature soared well above one hundred degrees; the kid working next to him was Jess Hall's own grandson, also named Larry. Clearly, Jess was not giving any soft breaks to family members. This is the same Larry Hall who later became Dad's trusted LSD guru and the man to whom Dad had mistakenly entrusted the care of his children in the early days of *Jeannie*.

I remember going to Big Jess's house once when I was a kid; he had very kind eyes and seemed like a real family man. It was Christmastime, and the big, dark, old house was imposing and a bit scary. The enormous Christmas tree loomed over the somber Victorian sitting room that was filled with heavy, dark wooden furniture. This brief encounter was the only time I can remember meeting Jess Hall Sr., so I did some research on him to better understand the impression this man had made on my father.

The three Hall brothers had moved to Weatherford, Texas, in 1941 to manufacture and sell the equipment that Jess had invented for improving oil drilling. In time, Mr. Hall held twenty-one American patents. The most popular piece of equipment he sold cost $1.75 to make; he sold it for $28.60. Back in 1947, right around the time my dad worked for the company, they sold hundreds of thousands of dollars' worth of this equipment to oil-drilling outfits in Venezuela. Eleven years later, Jess Hall Sr. was taken to court for tax evasion on the profits he gained in that foreign transaction. I read the court documents about the case, and there had been foreign companies set up to deal with payments in Venezuela and Puerto Rico, companies owned by various third parties as well as one of Hall's sons. In the end, through a long and winding path of companies changing hands, Jess Hall Sr. did not end up paying any back taxes. He must have been a very wise and cunning business-man, just the perfect role model on which to build the character of J. R.

With *Dallas*, Dad saw a second chance to mold a TV show into something truly memorable as he had with *I Dream of Jeannie*, but this time, he was determined to be careful not to alienate anyone.

In the first scripts for *Dallas*, J. R. was not a major character. His prominence in the Ewings' story would come later, after he'd developed a character that was so cunningly, forcefully, and physically charis-matic that television viewers around the world became captivated by him. Maybe Dad sensed J. R.'s potential, because after reading the *Dallas* script, he told Mom, "Mine's not the main part, but I think I can go someplace with it."

On the first day of shooting, he showed up on the *Dallas* set with a big smile on his face and Western saddlebags thrown over his shoulder filled with champagne. He charmed everyone. He was diplomatic and delightful to work with. This said, Dad was still rewriting dialogue right on the set like he had on *Jeannie*. But he did not lose his temper insisting on better scripts. Instead, he was constantly joking around with his fellow actors, using humor and a great deal of style and class to persuade people to change the direction of the show. He subtly moved it from a *Romeo and Juliet*–style drama about the marriage of young lovers from rival families, Bobby Ewing and Pamela Barnes, to a story about siblings in a rivalry for family power and money.

Once again, Dad was lucky: he had the best and most willing actors and companions to work with. Linda Gray and Patrick Duffy delighted in his practical jokes and were eager to take any suggestions he could offer that would give *Dallas* that Texas personality that only a true Texan could. Soon, the producers saw the public wanted more J. R. Everyone wanted to be him or be with him; he was the man they loved to hate.

J. R. didn't come out of the ether. The intensity everyone saw on-screen came from deep inside him. Dad would stare into the camera with this intense gaze, and his eyes would be twinkling with malice while he grinned his special grin that made him look as if he'd just eaten something wonderful and was savoring the taste of it in his mouth. Dad rarely got mad at me, but when he did, he would become very quiet and stare at me with that same look that had mesmerized viewers of the TV show. I got the full power of that gaze when it was riveted on me face-to-face; it could feel cold and hard and scary. Fans around the world saw these flashes of intensity as Dad looked straight into the camera and revealed his true and powerful personality. That personality had been forged by the burning need to surpass his mother and to finally prove to his strong, industrious wife that he could "bring home the bacon." Which he certainly did!

Money changed him. Instead of talking all the time about how broke he was, he reminded everyone about how rich he was. He bought Mom anything she wanted: a Rolls-Royce, every piece of jewelry she laid her eyes on. He sent Mom and me to Milan to sit in front-row seats at fashion shows and pick out designer clothes. Mom did not have to fix the plumbing herself anymore; in fact, they tore the whole house down so she could rebuild it without having to scrimp and save, and when she ran out of room in Malibu, he bought her forty acres in Ojai so she could continue building her dream house.

He was generous with my brother and me too, buying us our own homes and taking us on trips to Europe and flying our family around in private jets. He still espoused the mantra he had developed when the chips were down—DON'T WORRY! BE HAPPY! FEEL GOOD!—and he did everything he could to make us happy.

You would think that after having his greatest dreams come true he would have been able to relax; instead, he became super hyper. He would turn on the TV and the stereo and have both of them blasting while he was talking on the phone. It became more and more difficult to have a conversation with him. When he was not working on *Dallas,* he and Mom were always jetting off somewhere. I marveled at their energy and restlessness. The money was pouring in with sponsorships and talking gigs on top of his work on the show. Yet no matter how wealthy he got, his attitude about money was still colored by that period of tough love that Mary and Richard had imposed on him when he was a young actor, and they had kept him on a shoestring budget in the hope that Dad would not spend what little he had on booze. So even after he was making loads of money, it became clear that the memory of the frugality he'd experienced throughout his early days as a hungry young actor had left him feeling that he would never have enough and he would always be afraid of losing what he had.

He hired business managers to handle his contracts and financial affairs but seldom trusted them. It was his nature to socialize with people who worked for him, and he became close friends with some of them, but no matter how loyal they were, Dad was frightened of being take advantage of, and if he felt a shadow of doubt about someone's loyalty, he would cut that person out of his life forever. A very choice remained. Old habits die hard and even after his success in *Dallas,* he still could be seen stuffing dinner rolls in his pockets whenever he went to a party.

We knew J. R. had really caught on with the public because suddenly, wherever we went, there were big crowds. When we ate in restaurants, fans pressed against the windows to get a glimpse of him. Italy was one of those countries where J. R. was especially popular. I had spent some time in Italy during the summer between my junior and senior years of high school, and when we arrived there, I wanted to show my family the Florence I had discovered while traveling on my own. But as we walked through the streets, mobs of schoolchildren would march after us gleefully chanting, "J. R.! J. R.! J. R.!"

I was frustrated that our intimate family time was being violated, but Dad loved it; he smiled and patted the kids on their heads and handed out his fake hundred-dollar bills imprinted with the words "The United States of Texas" and "In Hagman We Trust."

Sometimes all this attention felt dangerous. Mom, Preston, and I would huddle around him to protect him, and he let us know that was our role. Whenever we headed out in public, he would say, "Get ready, family, for shark-feeding syndrome."

We would watch as Dad stepped out of the hotel onto the sidewalk, and moments later, we stepped in between him and the crowds because he was surrounded by people trying to touch him; it really was like Dad was fresh meat being thrown into a pool of frenzied sharks.

Though his fears about impending poverty did not change, his wardrobe did. Gone were the Engineer Bill striped overalls and tie-dyed shirts. Instead, he took to another sartorial extreme. Sometimes, he would dress as J. R., which meant elegant cowboy businessman attire, and that included Brooks Brothers suits, pointed boots, Stetson hats, a giant gleaming engraved belt buckle, and, to add his own quirky touch, custom hand-tooled leather saddlebags slung over his shoulder. Or sometimes he would get really crazy and wear a chicken suit or an outfit he developed over time that he called his pimp suit and consisted of a deep purple polyester suit and shockingly bright-yellow shirt worn with a tie decorated with a design of multicolored condoms.

He had always been class conscious; now he was more so. He spoke of certain people as being "below the salt," a term from the Middle Ages when saltcellars were placed in the center of the aristocracy's dining tables and the lowest-ranked people sat below that point. Mom and Dad were both fascinated by the British aristocracy. When they lived in London, they had both been in their twenties, and the country had made a huge impression on them. England was where they became adults. In addition to being where they fell in love, it was where they made some of their dearest lifelong friends. Before Mom met Dad, she had slept outside Buckingham Palace so she could see Princess Elizabeth on the way to her coronation to be queen.

My parents loved all the trappings and rituals of upper-class British society; they were overjoyed when Dad's dear friend and business partner Philip Mengel got them an invitation to the royal enclosure at the Ascot races. Mom wore a spectacular hat and an elegant pastel-colored suit, and Dad wore a proper morning suit and the requisite top hat. But there was a business aspect to their attendance and finery: Dad was up for a new *Dallas* contract, and Philip was handling the negotiations. The timing was perfect: the "Who shot J. R.?" episode had recently aired, and the TV-watching world was waiting to get the news about whether or not J. R. was dead and which one of his many enemies had shot him.

Dad and Philip used this worldwide attention to their advantage.

There were no cell phones then, and Dad was never quick to answer calls from the TV executives. Instead, he was making news, looking *fabulous* at the Royal Ascot races, which were being covered by the international press. Thanks to Philip Mengel's brilliant maneuvering, Larry Hagman became the best-paid actor on television.

I am sure Dad would say that one of the great high points of the *Dallas* years was when he and Ganny were invited to do a Royal Variety Performance in London honoring the Queen Mother's eightieth birthday. We were all so excited, and I felt very lucky to be with them; I was Ganny's roommate. She never went anywhere alone and had never been without Richard or someone hired to handle all the practical aspects of her life. She did not know how to call a cab or tip the room service waiter, so on this trip, because Richard had died several years before, I was appointed to take care of her. This was the first time I was given this sort of responsibility, and I took my job very seriously. I went everywhere with them and watched all the rehearsals.

In the show, Henry Mancini and his orchestra would play as Dad sang a song written especially for the show about his dastardly character J. R. Though the music had a faintly Western aspect, the structure of the song was vaguely similar to the song from *Peter Pan* about Captain Hook, who was the meanest and most despicable character imaginable. It went like this:

Who's the swiniest swine in world?
(Captain Hook! Captain Hook!)
Who's the dirtiest dog in this wonderful world?
(Captain Hook! Captain Hook!)

Dad's lyrics were based on them: "Who's a scoundrel? Who's a cheat? I am! I'm J. R.!"

At the rehearsal, he was singing by himself onstage, and then he started mumbling; he could not come up with the next line of the song, and he was having a hard time remembering the next terrible adjective to describe J. R. He was lost. Seeing his anxiety, Ganny came onstage before her cue to rescue him. She was dressed in one of her costumes from *South Pacific:* an absurdly gigantic, oversized sailor outfit. She was the perfect counter to the devilish J. R.; she was funny, naughty, and cute. As they practiced together, Dad became stiffer and stiffer. His nervousness just got worse; he had not sung onstage for a very long time, and though it was one of those songs that was more talking than singing, it was clear that he simply couldn't remember his lines. Ganny on the other hand was right in her element, relaxed and confident and completely at ease. They continued to work on the song as the rest of the cast watched from the audience. Ganny kept getting laughs as she attempted to get Dad to loosen up. She rubbed his shoulders and grabbed onto his hips to wiggle them around. Dad knew that no matter how ridiculous he might look, one of the best ways to capture the audience was to make them laugh, so in rehearsal, they worked out some playful business together about each one of them trying to one-up the other. It was funny, but it was also very close to the truth. I could tell Dad was on edge all day, so I ran his lines with him in his dressing room while Ganny had her hair done. Despite my youth, and given my role of caregiver for Ganny, I was like a mother figure to them both. I got him warm tea for the sore throat he had suddenly come down with, and I carried Ganny's purse for her.

During the show, when the curtain went up, J. R./Dad proudly walked onstage, and when he raised his Stetson while greeting the crowd, his fake J. R. dollars came streaming out as the audience broke up laughing. He hit his mark, but as the orchestra played the intro to his song, he went blank. He turned to Mr. Mancini and asked him to start from the beginning again. He did, but Dad was paralyzed, turning beet red and finally apologizing to the audience, saying, "I knew something like this would happen to me up here tonight. My daughter is in the audience."

I've never known why he said that or why my presence would make him more nervous than usual. Maybe he just needed someone to blame for his nerves, or since it was a show to celebrate a grandmother's eightieth birthday, maybe he was appealing to everyone in the audience who had ever gotten embarrassed in front of their kids. Finally, laughing because there was nothing else to do, he said, "I knew I would blow it! And what a place to blow it too!"

At last, on the third try, he got the song going, and when Ganny came out, she gave him a playful hip bump and stole the show. She took command, moving him around, and loosening him up. By the end of the piece, they were having a grand time, and the love and warmth between them was very real. It turned out to be a great night, and they made all the headlines the next day. One paper carried a cartoon of the Queen Mum standing up in her box with a rifle pointed at J. R. onstage, and he had his hands up, saying, "Don't shoot, Mum."

Dad was most happy and comfortable when he got the attention of strangers. Being famous fit him well, but eventually and inevitably, even J. R. faded from the spotlight. He still has very devoted fans, but when *Dallas* was off the air for several years, the crowds were not gathering around him as he went out in public. He really missed getting lots of attention as he made plain during one particular trip he made to Seattle, where I was living with my husband and two daughters.

He had come to visit us and do a Q and A with the theater class at my daughter Kaya's high school. Dad was not a teacher, and he did not know how to engage a high school class; he was accustomed to crowds that were eager to see him, crowds that knew all his work and laughed at all his jokes. These kids were too young to have a clue about *Dallas* and much too young to have seen *I Dream of Jeannie*.

It was a tough afternoon. The students didn't ask him many questions. The drama teacher and I prompted the kids into some kind of interaction with Dad, but the class wrapped up rather quickly, and there was polite applause at the end. Dad was accustomed to a big send-off. As we walked away from the school, I could sense his deflated ego with each step we took toward Pike Place Market, one of the biggest tourist draws in Seattle. No one was recognizing him there either. He was going up to vendors making small talk and joking around, but no one said, "Hey, aren't you that guy . . ." This brought him down even more. I saw the smile he had put on as he entered the market fading. I thought he might be hungry and tried to get him into a café for lunch, but he was determined to get a reaction out of the folks around him. Attention was the food he needed, and he figured out a way to get it. He bought a three-foot-long, bright-red, sequined beanbag lizard that he draped on his shoulder as if it were a live pet. This attracted the eyes of passersby, and when they took a moment to look at him, they would stop and say, "Aren't you J. R.?"

Then he would turn to them, his eyes twinkling, and say, with a devilish grin, "Why, yes, darlin', I am."

After that, he felt a lot better.

16

—

Real Life

M Y FIRST MARRIAGE ONLY LASTED two years. The wedding
took place during the height of the *Dallas* craze. Everything
was done on a grand scale; we announced our engagement at the
Rockefellers' estate. Our public life and private life had become a blur;
my wedding got a lot of publicity and fed the image that Dad was
proud to perpetuate. His dalliances notwithstanding, he was a very
loving family man, and he wanted the world to know this about him.
It was an image that was always very important to him.

My wedding had the same down-home family touch that all our
parties had. Mom and my aunts did the decorations and flowers and
supervised the food. A few hundred people attended, all crammed
into the newly built house in Malibu. The guest list included a lot of
people I did not know very well, like everyone who worked on *Dallas*,
from the stars to the script supervisor and costume people.

Mom had sewn my beautiful satin-and-lace dress. Ganny sang;
Aunt Heller's youngest children were the flower girl and ring bearers.

My godsister, Bridget Fonda, and one of my dearest girlfriends, Phillipa McNabb, were my bridesmaids, but even with all this love around me, it felt like we were putting on a show and the real stars were Dad and Ganny. I was so uncomfortable as I was getting dressed that, like many a bride before me, I almost called it off. Uncle Henri, who had been Dad's best man back in London, told me to pull myself together and gave me a Valium. I was looped and pale when I said my vows; Valium was another drug that was too strong for me. I will never know what I might have done that day without it.

The event was a great success from Dad's perspective: there were dozens of paparazzi to take pictures of our smiling family; they even came in helicopters to film the wedding from overhead, and there was Dad, in his element, the center of everything. For me, looking back on it, the dearest things are the family pictures in which Dad is just beaming, holding me close, and looking so happy, the proud patriarch at his daughter's wedding.

When I married again ten years later, it was no accident that I chose a man who had lived in Japan for the previous eight years. Daniel didn't know anything about what was happening in American popular culture, and that meant that he not only didn't care about J. R., he had never even heard of him!

Daniel's first window into what life is like for the family of a celebrity came during a trip we all took together to Turkey, where we were hounded by photographers and Dad encouraged him to shield us from them. Even after we were married, no matter how much distance we put between our new family and my father's fame, we could not really feel free from it. For example, we lived in Italy for six months so I could paint the landscape and Daniel could write and all of us, including our one-year-old daughter, could learn some Italian. Daniel had gotten in the habit of picking up old Italian magazines so he could practice reading in the language. He found one at an inn where we were staying in Rome. The magazine was filled with photos of my first wedding taken from the helicopter. There was even a picture of it on the cover; it was surreal. I had thought I had distanced myself from that tabloid reality and had built my own life far away from Dad's fame. But this incident made me realize that no matter how far away I go and no matter how much time passes, my family's fame is a part of my legacy whether I want it or not.

Another constant element of life for anyone connected to my family was joining the party and drinking. Daniel had seen my family getting drunk a lot. The first thing anyone did after entering my parents' house was to get a drink, and every meal was consumed with many bottles of wine. When we'd been dating for a while, Daniel told me he wanted me to stop drinking for three months because he did not want to get seriously involved with an alcoholic. After not drinking for a while, I had a different perspective on my family's rituals. Though I went back to drinking wine with dinner, I became much more aware of how insidious it could be. I've been more careful about my drinking ever since.

A little over a year after we met, Daniel and I decided to have a child. When I became pregnant, we were not yet married, and Dad was uneasy about the direction my life was taking. Hippie life and Swedish mores were not enough to make him comfortable with my having a child out of wedlock, but nothing he said was changing my mind about having this baby. When I was five months pregnant, I came by myself to Los Angeles for a visit with my parents. The first night, during dinner, Dad and Mom and other family members were all drinking heavily. I was sober, of course. Dad and my uncle began joking about attending the birth of my child. This was at a time when families had just begun filming births. They were going on and on about how they would video the birth. They were all laughing about where the camera would be placed and making innuendos about porn films and teasingly referring to the noises I would make while giving birth. As I sat there I started envisioning my delivery room filled with my drunken, rowdy family all making fun of me instead of the intimate, important moment I longed for, during which I would bring a new life into the world. I knew they had no understanding of what this meant to me, and this was not the time to tell them about how I wanted my birthing experience to be, so I excused myself from the table, saying I was tired, and went upstairs to my room.

I had just crept into bed and taken my contact lenses out when my mother came through the door, which was three steps up from the sunken bedroom. She was very drunk by then, and she was yelling, reminding me of all the things she and Dad had given me. Who did I think I was anyhow? Did I think Daniel's family was better than my own because they all had college degrees? She was so out of control, she was not really making any sense, so I stayed in bed and asked her to leave, but she wouldn't go. I could not make out her facial expression without my contacts, so in order to see her better, I finally got out of bed and went up the three steps and stood close to her. I said, "Mom, you have to let me go to sleep."

She pushed me. I fell backward. It was only three steps, but I hit my back hard. Finally, she left the room. That night, I started bleeding.

The next morning, I told my aunt BB about the blood, and she immediately arranged for me to see a doctor. Dad insisted on taking me. It was about ten in the morning, and he drove me to the hospital on a beautiful sunny day in the Mustang convertible with the top down. He was trying to lighten the mood with music, and the wind whipped my hair around, which on any other occasion might have been fun, but I was hurting and very worried about the possibility of losing the baby. Looking over at Dad, I could see that he was shaking. I had seen him with the DTs before, and I knew he hadn't had a drink yet that morning the way he usually did. He calmed himself by sucking on some hard candy, which helped control his need for sugar, which the booze ordinarily supplied. He never mentioned anything that had been said the night before or how Mom had behaved.

He was visibly relieved when the doctor said all I needed was to be on bed rest for the next few weeks. She reassured us the baby and I would be okay.

Dad had watched as the doctor did the ultrasound. He saw the baby open her fingers as if she were waving. He was enchanted . . . his grandchild had waved at him. Now he could rewrite the story of what had brought us to the hospital that day. It was no longer the story of a frightening episode in which Mom, in a drunken rage, had put her grandchild in jeopardy. All that faded away as Dad put a positive spin on the event and made himself the focus of a story that was now about how he had taken care of his daughter, who was having trouble with her pregnancy, and how he had been the first person in the family to see his new grandchild. "I saw my baby grandchild," Dad proudly told everyone, "and she waved at me."

When it came time for me to give birth, Daniel and I agreed that my family should not attend. We had talked a lot about what had happened in LA and all the drinking. We had gone to birthing classes and read books about creating a peaceful, healthy birth, and we did not want that birth influenced in any way by their hard-drinking party energy. However, we did want the support of some family members, so we asked Daniel's father, who was a psychiatrist, to be with us throughout the birth. In retrospect, I think my parents felt I had chosen Daniel's family over them at this important moment in our lives, and the message they got was that I was taking some distance from them.

A week after my daughter was born, Mom came to visit without Dad, who was working and couldn't get away. She brought presents for the baby. She was warm toward me, cordial to Daniel, and thrilled to see baby Kaya. But it was clear that my insistence on taking control of the way my daughter was born had strained the very strong connection my parents and I had always had. But thinking back on it, difficult and unpleasant as the events surrounding my pregnancy were, my father would not have seen them as anything for which he needed to be forgiven.

17

Parents

Dad never did anything around the house. He never changed lightbulbs or cleaned dishes or paid bills. One day, long after *Dallas* had ended, we were getting ready for a big luncheon at his immense and gorgeous estate in Ojai. The wind had picked up the night before, and the gardener did not have time to come back to the house to clear away the leaves and debris that were scattered all over the terrace. Before setting the table, I got out a broom and began sweeping, Dad picked up another broom that was leaning against the wall and started sweeping too. He was awkward with the broom and said to me, "I don't think I've ever done this before."

I paused and looked at him, not sure if he was being sarcastic or not; then I thought to myself, he must have swept a floor before, but the truth is, it may have been decades since he had picked up a broom because, as he would say, "I have people to do that for me."

He was good at getting help. If he could not figure out how to use the remote control on his TV, he would hire someone to do it; other people washed the cars, grew the vegetables, typed and sent the letters he dictated, and on and on, and they all loved doing it for him. Often, he paid for these services, but he was known for getting people to do things for him for free. He would talk to them and genuinely admire their ability. Dad was flattering me by telling me he did not know how to sweep a floor; he was acknowledging that I regularly did something he did not do.

Mom, on the other hand, as I've noted, did not hesitate to get right in there and do all sorts of things herself. That's not to say she didn't have household help: she always had as much help as we could afford, but she never ceased to enjoy cooking and cleaning and fixing things. The longer they were married, the more Dad came to depend on her to manage their day-to-day lives, and she was his helpmate in all decisions. He would hate this comparison, but their arrangement was very much like the one Ganny had had with Richard: there was an unspoken agreement in both relationships that enabled both Larry and Mary the freedom to be artists while their partners helped craft their image and manage things behind the scenes. Mom, in addition to doing many of the household repairs herself or, if not, finding the right person for the job, also mended and altered Dad's clothes for him; until she became completely confused, she could sew anything. For years, if Dad bought a shirt he really liked, Mom would take it apart and make a pattern; she would then improve on the garment and make a dozen of them for him in every color. Even after their ship came in with the success of *Dallas,* she and her sisters continued to do a lot of the daily cooking. Mom managed all the details of running their Santa Monica and Ojai households, the latter of which was twenty thousand square feet, had three pools, and had six permanent employees. She packed for their trips abroad and took everything they needed; Dad was good at putting his toiletries bag together and delighted in planning the outfits he wanted to wear, including special hats for each one, but it was Mom who made sure all the practical stuff was there. She packed in such a way that the clothes would not wrinkle. They traveled a great deal, and experience had taught her how to arrange things so it would be easy to find the coats they would need at the end of a long trip that would start with a warm week in Florida and end with a visit to Moscow during the winter. She knew just where to go to buy anything they needed, from plumbing fixtures to Georgian silver tea sets.

Because she had taken care of him in every possible way, when she became too ill to do that, Dad was miserable and adrift. I began to understand just how lost he was when his appliances started breaking down. Short of hiring experts, he did not have a clue about what to do when something broke. It seemed foolish to find an "expert" to fix his toaster, so he asked me, "Where do you go to buy a toaster?"

This was a simple question, but it told me that he never had to think about these sorts of practical everyday things before.

Another aspect of their lives that Mom had handled was their real estate and financial concerns. She and Dad would meet with the investment advisors and accountants, and when they got home, she would talk everything over with Dad; invariably, she would need to calm him down because talking about money engendered so much anxiety in him and often caused him to feel that they did not have enough cash to cover their costs. Mom was confident and practical. She knew they were well off, while Dad, to the end of his days, and even when there was loads of evidence to the contrary, could not help but worry that something terrible would happen by the end of the year that would leave him totally broke again.

Mom's amazing array of talents included the ability to read the architectural plans for the homes they built and buildings they bought.

Aging did not modify her innate restlessness, and throughout her life, she would always need something to do. Dad said he liked paying for construction workers because then Mom would have other men to order around.

After Mom had rebuilt their home in Malibu several times and needed more space to create, they moved to Upper Ojai, a picturesque town that looks like a mini Santa Fe and is a two-hour drive north of Malibu. The move to Ojai presented Mom with the ideal situation: a place where she could design and build to her heart's content on a forty-acre site on the top of a mountain overlooking the ocean.

The Mediterranean home she envisioned and built was an amazing place with beautiful foliage and trees. It had several pools that flowed all through the house and ended as a moat around Dad's den. The den was beneath the book-filled Victorian-style library, and you got to it by going behind voluminous silk curtains that revealed an elegant spiral staircase from which you could look onto Dad's moat. At the base of the stairway, there was a retractable metal door that turned his inner sanctum into a hidden fortress. Inside, Mom had decorated his hideout like a fantasy creation from an Arab fairy tale that Jeannie would have felt at home in: there were Persian carpets and Oriental antiques and, amid all this finery, a walk-in safe full of guns and ammo. That was the only really private space in the house; the rest of it was designed as a party palace with nine bedrooms in four separate towers.

Between the towers was the huge eat-in kitchen and, next to it, the dining room with an enormous round table (no one was below the salt here). The walls were covered with hand-painted murals of the desert. Down a long hallway that looked like it came from a medieval monastery, you got to the billiards room where there was a huge bed and big couches and high-backed chairs and a big-screen TV. Above this playroom there were two more sleeping towers with many bathrooms.

There was also the part of the house they called "the Pavilion," which was a huge space the size of three tennis courts put together that had three large seating areas, a grand piano, and a loft with workout equipment. It included a large indoor pool with a cascading fountain flowing into it that had been inspired by one my parents had seen in Istanbul when we had all visited the last sultan's palace, now a museum. Dad was particularly struck by the idea that the fountain where the harem had been kept was built so that secrets spoken there would be masked by the sound of the trickling water, and he wanted one of his own. Just to the side of the pool there was a cave-like Jacuzzi. The pool could be covered for big parties to create a dance floor, and just as we had in Malibu, there was a mirrored ballroom ball that spun, suspended high above with a spotlight that sent sparkles dancing all over the space when the industrially powerful sound system blasted out everything from Strauss waltzes to The Moody Blues.

The Pavilion was surrounded by giant glass doors that opened to a view of the ocean on one side and to an inner courtyard with more pools and fountains on the other. The crowning feature of this grand room was an eight-foot-by-twenty-five-foot retractable skylight. Mom had made sure that this place had everything Dad ever desired. When it was completed, he named it Heaven because it was the one kind of heaven he emphatically believed in: heaven on earth.

Mom believed you could do anything you set your mind to, and Dad tested her abilities. One morning during one of the many times in our lives when he was obsessing about being broke, he started thinking about what he would like if he were really rich. He tried to think of the most outrageous, impossible thing one could have for breakfast. Finally, he said, "I want Baked Alaska."

Mom liked the challenge, and she sent me to the grocery store with a list of things to buy. An hour later, she served the Baked Alaska to him in bed, on a silver tray. It was a gorgeous confection: frothy golden-brown meringue on the outside with layers of ice cream and cake inside. Though Mom did not have Dad's earning capacity, nor did she get anything even approaching the recognition he received, my father always knew that she was something of a magician when it came to making dreams come true.

The image of the Swedish sex goddess was very prevalent in the '60s and '70s. There was the Swedish actress Anita Ekberg from the Fellini movie *La Dolce Vita* and the "take it off, take it all off" blonde from the Noxzema shaving cream commercial on TV. Dad was proud to have his very own Swede. She was strong, blond, and direct. He was wildly amorous toward her for much of his life. They were very physically comfortable together, holding each other's hands and kissing in public; he could always make her giggle. When I was still a toddler in New York, Mom was painting the walls of our apartment when Dad grabbed the brush from her and wrote in letters two feet tall, "I love you, Honey Bunny." She never painted over it. Instead, she covered it with a curtain, and whenever she needed to cheer herself up, she would pull back the curtain and read it again or proudly show friends this giant-sized declaration of Dad's love.

He liked her to be dressed well, and even when money was in short supply, she could sew an evening gown for herself that would rival anything seen on the Oscars' red carpet. Dad remembered details about her dresses years after she'd worn them. He especially loved the Dior look; to him, it supplied the quintessential image of a beautiful woman. Mom was determined to please him. I once overheard a friend of the family say that she'd had a rib removed so she could wear the Dior cinched-in waists or the exaggerated hourglass look with its tight built-in corsets and voluminous skirts. She was stunning in them, and

Dad was so proud of her. He always liked to walk behind her so he could see her legs in her high heels.

She was aware of her image as the woman accompanying a famous actor, and she put a lot of time into thinking about how she presented herself. She did not hesitate to do whatever it took to make herself attractive, be it in the clothes she wore, or dieting intensely to quickly get thin for a gala, or exploring anything plastic surgery could do to improve her looks.

Dad had fallen in love with her soon after she had suffered from polio and was never troubled by the way the left side of her face dropped slightly from nerve damage caused by the disease. But even after she'd had that epiphany about her face when they took acid together and she had said, "I'm beautiful," she remained very self-conscious about her crooked mouth and tried many times to correct it with dentistry and half a dozen face-lifts over the years. Dad supported and encouraged her as she often turned to doctors to improve her body, especially during the heyday of *Dallas*. To her credit, Mom also did everything she could on her own to stay in shape during those years and put Dad on a workout and diet regimen; when she was fifty, she was running eight miles a day and lifting weights with Arnold Schwarzenegger.

Despite all Mom's efforts, something went wrong. The blissful marriage my folks always presented to the public had a sad, hidden side. I did not wake up to this fact until one day in the late 1980s, when my parents were living in LA and I was in New York painting. Mom called me in my studio; she was crying. She called often; we were very close and talked about everything. We loved to gossip together. In these conversations, she was often boastful, angry, or elated, but hearing her sound so miserable was very unusual. I wanted to

211

comfort her in any way I could. When she finally caught her breath between sobs, she told me that Dad was not intimate with her anymore. I was silent for a long while. If I were there in California with her, I would have hugged her, but what could I do over the phone? I said, "Mom, maybe it's the drinking that makes him this way."

She said, "No, that's not the problem; you have to say something to him."

How could I say anything to my father about their sex life? I felt really uncomfortable saying anything to either of them. She wanted to go on telling me things about their personal life that I did not want to hear, and she was putting Dad down in very explicit terms, but as close as I was to my mother, I was not her girlfriend. As daughter to both of them, I finally said, "I cannot have this conversation with you. I really don't want to know those kinds of details about your life together."

After that phone call, I intentionally turned a blind eye to much of my parents' life together. I never really wanted to look too deeply. Dad was always a flirt, but it was done with such good humor that I never took it seriously. But since his death, I've been confronted repeatedly with the fact that he had many affairs. Just a week ago, I was talking to a friend of Dad's about the woman who was with him at his deathbed, and the man asked, "You mean that woman he saw every day on his way to work?" Once again, there I was, tripping over another revelation of a liaison that was altogether news to me. All I could do was pretend I already knew. I needed some time to process the information, so I just said yes and changed the subject.

After Mom developed Alzheimer's, I found myself covering for Dad even though I did not really know what he was up to. For example, I was Dad's date at a charity function in Dallas when a very respectable couple who were friends with both my parents asked me, "How can you put up with it?" as they gestured to a group of women that

Dad often traveled with and who were, at that moment, hovering around him.

I just said, "It comes with the territory; famous people need a lot of love." But I was not really sure what these women were to my father. It was one of those situations in which I did not want to ask too many questions. I figured Dad's relationships were his business.

To my knowledge, the first time my mother confronted Dad about his other women was when they visited my family in Santa Fe, New Mexico. I had listened to Daniel's counsel and continued to maintain some distance between my parents and myself. For the first time in my life, I did not feel like a member of the family entourage. I had forged a new family and become an artist in my own right. In Santa Fe, people did not care very much about the whole J. R. connection, which allowed me to live my own way. I was painting and learning the craft of printmaking alongside the many kind and generous artists who lived and worked in my community. I was very happy. Daniel and I were looking forward to seeing Mom and Dad and showing the grandparents what a strong, curious, beautiful granddaughter they had.

As soon as Mom walked through the door, I could see she was distraught and that this was not going to be a kid-focused visit. Dad was unusually subdued and followed behind her quietly. They sat in our living room, ignoring their granddaughter, and through her tears, Mom told us that there had been a story in the supermarket tabloids about my father having an affair. I never saw the article and never cared to; I did not know anything about this other woman and did not feel like finding anything out, but it was all too clear that for Mom this news and the public nature of it was devastating and humiliating. Between bursts of sobbing, she said, "I need you to be family. I need us to stick together to overcome this horrible intrusion into our lives."

Here we were again, just like the phone call I'd had with Mom a few years earlier. What could I do? Dad was Dad. The tabloids were always picking on people and poking around for dirt; this is the price that comes with fame. As we sat there listening to Mom, Dad did not say a word. I did not know what the tabloid had reported. I did not even want to look for it on the newsstands, and I had no intention of asking my father if it was true or not.

I told her, "If we don't say anything, if we just keep quiet, it will blow over. It will be a passing thing. It's just one moment of sensationalism. No one believes those tabloids anyway." Dad looked at me helplessly as if he just wanted to hand Mom over to someone else. The tension was unbearable. Dad opened a bottle of wine—his answer to most tense situations—but Mom was too miserable to be consoled. I focused on my toddler, who had become agitated, sensing the atmosphere in the room.

I know he must have felt bad, but Dad just kept smiling. As the day wore on, he went out to a bar to get away and drink with the locals. He stayed out on the town for a long time, and he figured that while he was gone, Mom would have some drinks too and that things would cool down by the time he came home. He truly did love my mother, and it pained him to see her this way. He wanted to do something to distract her and change her mood. Finally, he decided on a plan that would defuse the situation and then went wandering around town looking for the ingredients he needed. First, he looked for a silly hat, one that he would soon add to his huge hat collection. Santa Fe was full of hat stores, and he found one he hoped would make my mother laugh: it was made of shearling and had two horns coming out of it like the horns of the devil. When he put it on, he looked like a creature from Maurice Sendak's children's book *Where the Wild Things Are*. He walked around the plaza wearing it, and people recognized him and asked for autographs.

Dad liked to make this kind of interaction unpredictable, and so he would ask the fans for something in return. People were stunned by his response. What could they give this big star who surely had everything he wanted and needed and then some? Dad would say, "For an autograph, you can sing to me or tell me a joke or recite a poem." This would produce embarrassed laughter and a lot of off-key singing of "Happy Birthday" or recitations of "Humpty Dumpty" or "Mary Had a Little Lamb." On this occasion, the songs and poems improved Dad's mood substantially, and then he passed a newsstand where he saw a *Time* magazine cover with a picture of a pig's head on the body of a man in a suit and the words: "Are Men Really That Bad?" It was as if the zeitgeist was in tune with his personal situation. Could the headline have been any more perfect?

Using the things he'd collected on his afternoon trip around Santa Fe, Dad found a unique way to apologize for the public humiliation my mother had suffered. He walked back into the house with his ever-present smile, which had looked so strained before he'd left. He was now genuinely happy. He had it all figured out, and as always, his good mood was infectious, and we wanted to help him make things better.

He got to work on his plan: after arranging the pillows on the living room couch, he stretched out on it, wearing the hat that made him look like a monster; then he got my husband to take a picture of him while he lay there grinning, holding a teddy bear in one hand and, in the other hand, the *Time* magazine with its cover line, "Are Men Really That Bad?"

This was Dad's way of charming everyone and making things okay. He could turn an upsetting situation into something funny. He had the ability to be self-deprecating or silly and humorous. He would make us all laugh, and if anyone stayed mad, that person looked like a spoilsport. This tactic very often worked, even when what he did or said was outrageous, like the time he was at a PTA meeting at my high school, where many parents had been terribly upset by rumors about sex between teachers and students. Students and teachers had gone skinny-dipping on a class trip, and there were whisperings of other, more serious interactions between teachers and students. Understandably, there was a great deal of anger expressed. Because Dad was always so uncomfortable with conflict, he wanted to defuse the situation. He stood up and said, "Now if you really want to do something to protect our kids, we should make emergency packs to be stored at all the exits of the school for them in case of an earthquake." And in the surprised silence created by his abrupt change of subject, he added, "We could even include some condoms in the packs for good measure."

Luckily, everyone laughed. Dad had performed his usual tactic of distracting people from their serious stance, and the meeting continued without addressing the issue of sex again. Another time, at a fancy dinner in Dad's honor, a child was scolded for talking with his mouth full. This must have reminded him of the way that Richard had always been on his case about table manners, so Dad turned to the boy's parents, crossed his eyes, and stuck his tongue out with food all over it. Again, there was laughter. He was the king of the court jesters, and, as the famous and infamous J. R., he could get away with doing something in egregiously bad taste and no one seemed to take offense. Dad liked to knock people off their high horses and grandiose attitudes.

At one point, we spent a week in Washington, D.C., where Ganny was to be one of the recipients of the Kennedy Center Honors. The whole time was filled with events lauding her and the other awardees. During a fancy brunch, Dad saw Katharine Graham turning heads as she entered the room. He came over to where I was seated to point her out to me and to explain that she was one of the most powerful women in America because she was the publisher of her highly influential family-owned paper, *The Washington Post*. Later that evening, he was seated next to her at dinner and, turning to her as he looked at her place card, he said, "Graham? Are you related to that preacher guy named Graham?"

She looked at him for a moment, regarding him silently, and seeing his ever-present smile, she could tell he was yanking her chain, and she had the good grace to laugh. For Dad, teasing Mrs. Graham in this way was his attempt to say, "In the end, none of us are all that important." It was Dad's version of speaking truth to power.

And, thinking back on that day in Santa Fe, Dad was rewriting how we would remember their visit. After having his picture taken, my mother had regained her composure and was smiling; no one talked about the article in the tabloid again. To this day, the remaining members of our family refuse to look at or talk about anything that hurts. It is a coping mechanism, but it is not a path to healing the wounds of a life spent in the eye of the public with fallible people for parents.

For a while, my mother found a way to make peace with the knowledge that Dad had other women. Though she didn't address it directly, the way she regarded such liaisons—and rationalized them—became clear when she spoke about women who demanded divorces from their cheating husbands. She said she felt sorry for them; they were pathetic and unsophisticated. She thought they should put up with their husbands' affairs, because if they lost their husbands, they would lose everything.

This attitude must have come from an agreement my parents came to privately, because from that time forward, Dad was more careful about crossing the line. Though he didn't stop having affairs, he conducted them in a way that would ensure that Mom was not embarrassed again by a public display of the women he hadn't kept properly hidden. He did a special interview titled "Love in Hollywood" that included a video of them walking hand in hand on the beach while they talked about their perfect marriage and how he had been faithful to her for forty years. The whole family was interviewed about how amazing they were together, and there is no doubt that they were amazing together, they always loved each other deeply. They were a great team. He was consistent in every interview and always spoke of his devotion to his wife; he liked to make the point that he was a bad boy in all things *except* marriage. When he wrote his autobiography, the book was full of confessions about his drug and alcohol use. He went into detail about every law he had ever broken, but he maintained that he was a faithful and loving husband.

As long as he kept up appearances, he could do anything he wanted with other women. But to remind him not to mess up again, he kept that picture of himself lying on the couch in Santa Fe wearing the monster hat with the *Time* cover in his hand. In fact, he had it framed and hung in the kitchen, where everyone could see it every day while they ate breakfast.

What he really felt about his affairs is something, I suspect, that nobody knows. But the more I thought about it and the further along I got in my forensic search for who my father was, I became ever more certain that those affairs were not the reason he had asked to be forgiven.

18

The Miracle of Medicine

It was the best of times. It was the worst of times . . .
—CHARLES DICKENS

DAD WAS DIAGNOSED WITH CIRRHOSIS of the liver in 1992. By then, his daily pattern was to start the morning with a beer or a vodka and orange juice and continue on by drinking beer and wine all day. He liked to quote W. C. Fields's line, "I don't drink water. Fish fuck in it."

He had been drinking heavily since he was fourteen. At first, it was a rebellion from the strict upbringing he had experienced in his grandmother's care and a reaction to the great pain of losing her and coming to live in a situation in which his stepfather made him feel unwelcome. Then, as a teenager in Texas, drinking was the way to get close to his father and stepmother. Next came his time in the service, putting on shows and going to all the clubs to find talent, where hard drinking was the norm. Returning to the United States in the late 1950s, he and Mom were on the fringe of Mary and Richard's social circle, a crowd who drank martinis as if they were drinking water.

Dad always said that when Jack Nicholson turned him on to marijuana, he was saved from becoming an alcoholic like his stepfather,
but the truth is he just added pot to the alcohol. So it was no huge
surprise that, at the age of sixty-one, he had to face the hard reality
that if he kept drinking, he would probably be dead within six months.
In interviews, he would always say that when he got this news, he
stopped drinking . . . just like that. No problem. He'd point out that
he had stopped smoking three packs of cigarettes a day and claimed
that this was proof that he did not have an addictive personality;
drinking was no different, right? But drinking *was* different. He tried
not to drink, but all his life he had been a happy drunk. And though
he did manage to cut down on his drinking just before his operation
and for about a year after it, he was visibly uncomfortable without his
booze. He was afraid that, without the booze, he would not be funny
anymore.

My mom did not stop drinking when Dad got his diagnosis, even
though she knew it was poison for him. She was addicted too and
must have been in denial about the effect her drinking might have on
Dad. I suppose she didn't want to drink alone, because she frequently
told him how good the wine tasted with a meal, and then she'd say,
"Why don't you have just a little sip or two, just to taste it?" Mom was
not a happy drunk; she got mean. Anyone who tried to get her to stop
drinking saw just how mean she could be.

Liver disease is not pretty. As Dad's liver began to fail, the whites of
his eyes turned yellow, his skin became sallow and his body puffy; his
normally prodigious energy was compromised. Dad had been a very
healthy man most of his life, but at this stage, whenever he came to
visit me in Santa Fe, he needed oxygen. He became resigned to his

new diminished capacity and was becoming disengaged from everyone around him; he did not seem to care about anything anymore. His positive attitude used to change everything. He had always been the ringleader, the leader of the pack, the one who was funny and charismatic and cheerful and happy. Now there was a void in our lives, and no one to lift us out of the sadness in which we were becoming mired.

Three years after his initial diagnosis, his doctor found a malignant tumor in his liver. The only way to save his life was a liver transplant. Before the operation, he became even more depressed and despondent. Maybe the detailed description of the liver transplant surgery was very scary for him. Maybe it was really hard not drinking, and he could not imagine living in a way that did not include a social life with drinking at its core. Maybe the disease had altered him so much that he no longer believed he could ever be his old happy self again. He almost didn't care whether or not he had the transplant. He had given up.

This was a time when I was more distant from my parents than I'd ever been before. And I was not the only person who had become alienated from them. In recent years, my mother had been so worried about Dad's deteriorating health that she was mean to everyone. Dad, who usually countered any of her bad moods, had been so withdrawn and depressed leading up to the surgery that he didn't seem to want anyone around, so I saw them just a few times a year.

Nothing we could say made him feel hopeful about the operation. Finally, what gave him the courage to go ahead with it was talking to someone who'd been there and done it. People on a list for a liver transplant were given sponsors, someone who had gone through the procedure and who could be supportive and answer any questions Dad might have. Dallas Taylor, the drummer for the band Crosby, Stills, and Nash, had had a liver transplant the year before. He and Dad began having long, serious conversations. Whoever picked Taylor for Dad was inspired. He was just the right person for the job because Dad's considerable drug use was nothing compared to Taylor's, and that gave Taylor street cred in Dad's eyes. Taylor had gotten so caught up in drugs and alcohol that eventually his bandmates, no strangers to drugs themselves, would have nothing to do with him. He blew it. During the height of that drug-crazed era when everyone was doing a lot of drugs, he went too far. Taylor knew the depths of the destruction that substance abuse can cause and spent the rest of his life helping people beat addiction. He was compassionate with Dad in the way that only someone who truly knew how Dad was feeling could be, and he convinced Dad that he should have the transplant, assuring him that he could have a good, full life after the operation.

Dad was sitting on one of the terraces in Ojai gazing out at the ocean when the buzzer went off on his mobile device, signaling they had found a liver for him. There was no time to drive the winding roads to the hospital, so a helicopter landed on the seldom-used heliport, and he was whisked away to begin the long operation that gave him back his life. Transplants are talked about very casually these days, but it is a very difficult and transformative operation. He would be on an amazingly long list of drugs for the rest of his life. As much as he loved Ojai, he could not live there right after the operation; it was too far from the hospital. So his good friend Carroll O'Connor, who owned several houses and preferred to stay at his home in Malibu, suggested that Dad stay in his house in Westwood while he was recovering. A nursing team was hired to attend to him night and day; a huge hospital bed was placed in the very center of that room. Dad was ensconced there for weeks. Suspended just above his body was a giant chandelier that struck me as a hybrid of elegance and hippie mystic crystal healing power. Only my mom and Aunt BB and a very select few friends were allowed to visit and attend to him.

Dad was prescribed antirejection drugs, which made him feel omnipotent. He watched the U.S. Open on TV and was convinced he was controlling every move the players made with the power of his mind. He told everyone that he could make the tennis pros win or lose, that he was in complete control of all the games being played. He ordered Mom and Aunt BB around. He designed a new bedside lamp and got my aunt, who had a furniture factory, to have a dozen lamps made to his specifications. He bought a magnificent penthouse condo in Santa Monica. He furiously dictated letters to his secretary and had Mom sew new clothes for him. His energy was back! More than back—the drugs had made him even more manic than he'd ever been.

My mother waited on him every minute of the day. Having always been completely dedicated to him, she was even more so in those difficult months when he was recovering.

When I went to his bedside, I was five months pregnant with my second child. There was still a lot of tension between my parents and me that had begun when my mother pushed me down those three stairs, and it had worsened when I did not invite them to be present at my first daughter's birth. But I needed to see my dad, so, right after the operation, I asked politely if I could visit him with Kaya, my daughter who was then almost four years old. When we arrived, Dad was still very bruised, and much of his body was swollen to three times its normal size. Kaya was very brave and sensitive; she did not shy away from her grandfather, even though he was scary to look at. Instead, my tiny daughter courageously rubbed his distended ankles and sang to him soothingly. Her actions made me aware of her need to be connected with him and forced me to recognize his mortality.

The reality that Dad's days were numbered made me feel the need to become closer to my parents again. After that, I made the effort to bring all their grandchildren to see Dad and Mom as often as I could.

We were all having a new start. Dad had his new lease on life. Mom was happier and relieved that he was well. I had just moved with my family to Seattle in the hopes that Daniel, who was now my husband, would find good work, and I soon had my new baby in my arms, my lovely little Nora. Kaya was starting kindergarten. It was a good time to let old wounds heal and enjoy a new beginning.

Even so, whenever I brought my daughters to visit, I knew that I had to be very careful about letting the kids be alone with my mother because she was drinking a lot. Mom adored her grandchildren, and I made sure that all of them, including my brother's kids, spent a few weeks with them every year. But when the girls were visiting, I tried my best to not let them out of my sight. I did everything I could to make sure she did not drive them anywhere, but sensing and resenting the restrictions I'd put on her interaction with her granddaughters, Mom would find sneaky ways to take them in the car. Once when I was still in the shower, she loaded all the girls into her sports car. I could hear them yelling good-bye to me, so I ran out of the shower still dripping wet and wrapped in a towel. I yelled after Mom to bring them back, but my voice did not reach her, and I was left to watch and worry as they sped down the long, winding driveway to the main road.

Even without the problems my mother posed, it was hard keeping such young girls safe in that big house that was not childproofed in any way and had so many pools and towers. And, given all the lavish decorations and antiques, I had to protect the house from the kids too. One day, I was doing a painting project with them. We were working in the only room that was easy to clean up, at the very top of one of the towers. It had floors that would not be damaged by art materials. While we were working, one of the girls needed to go to the bathroom, and I was so distracted showing another of them how to draw a cat that I did not notice how much paint she had accumulated on her hands. She ran down the stairs to use my mother's private bathroom. She was gone a long time, and by the time I found her, she had wiped her paint-covered hands all over the red silk damask walls of the room.

She knew she had done something wrong and was so worried that Grandma would get mad at her. She was trying desperately to clean it off but was only making it worse. Fortunately, it was water-based paint, and I calmed her down as I cleaned the walls. We were away from the other girls for quite a while, and when I got back to them, they had piled up a bunch of the terrace furniture so they could climb over the railing to get into the top of a nearby tree. They were three stories up! I nearly had a heart attack. On that same visit, one of the girls was walking from the living room toward the indoor pool and saw a snake. Thank god she ran to Grandma Maj for help. When Mom came back with her and saw the rattler by the stairs, she got the little one out of the way. Though I often worried what she would do with so many glasses of wine in her system, I was glad that she acted without hesitation to protect the girls. She quickly found a machete in Dad's den and then swiftly returned to where the snake was and cut off its head.

All this convinced me that it was impossible to be with all the girls every minute, so the next time I visited with them, I brought a nanny. She was a sweet woman who had babysat for me in Seattle. I thought I could relax, but one morning as I was drinking my tea, I looked down the hallway to where the girls were playing on the decorative silver saddle that was on a stand by the entryway. The nanny was with them, and I smiled at them, but just then, the girl on the saddle reached into the gun holster that was slung over the horn of the saddle and pulled out the pistol and pointed it at my youngest! I screamed and ran down to where they were and gave the same lecture that I had repeated so many times before: "All the guns in this house are loaded. You never point a gun at anyone!"

The nanny was so shaken up by the experience that she took a Valium and went to bed. It was getting harder and harder to visit, and for a while, I did not let my girls sleep over anymore. Mom never stopped drinking until all her choices were taken away from her due to advanced vascular dementia, which could have been caused by her habit of drinking three or four bottles of wine a day and topping it off with a couple of vodkas before going to bed.

After Dad's operation, my mother continued to drink, but Dad stopped drinking entirely for a while. This was the first time in my life that I knew him sober. These months of his sobriety were very important to me. As loving and cuddly as he'd always been, for the first time I felt that he was actually listening to me and that he would remember what we had been talking about. More than at any other time before, I felt that he was genuinely interested in what I said. We had many in-depth conversations, but we seldom had personal talks. Even in his sobriety, that sort of intimacy was never going to happen; it made him squirm. Still, there was so much for us to discuss together: Dad was a voracious reader who subscribed to dozens of magazines, and through analyzing books, articles, and movies, we became closer. We talked about politics and global warming. He was always sending me books with titles like *The End of Oil*. While reading several of these books, we all bought Geo Metros, the smallest, most fuel-efficient cars on the market at the time. We also read novels together—Thomas Mann's *The Magic Mountain* and Barbara

Kingsolver's *The Poisonwood Bible*—and we discussed the authors and the time in history when the novels took place. We talked about the philosophical issues that emerged when we read these books: what happens to someone who lives in a country he or she did not grow up in, how the clash of cultures changes him or her, how you define culture, and on and on. He wanted to know what publications I read, and when I cited *The Utne Reader*, *The New York Review of Books*, and *The Nation*, he subscribed to all of them.

Sobriety changed him in other positive ways. He became even more attentive to his granddaughters, the Blondies, who had always been his playmates. Being sober did not stop him from being a lot of fun. He would go out and buy them all sorts of playful things. One day it would be big, red, bulbous clown noses, and he would set an example by wearing his out in public in an effort to encourage us all to put the red clown noses on too, which we did. Another time, he bought a bunch of big jellylike rings that had a battery inside that made the ring light up, flashing multicolored lights. He distributed these rings to the girls, and when he drove his electric car around Santa Monica, he used his ring to get the attention of other drivers when he made turn signals by hand.

Both my parents loved getting pictures that my kids drew and, later, the cards and letters they wrote as well as copies of their school report cards. I talked to them a lot about how important it was to get the best education that we could find for their grandchildren because the world had changed so much since they were young. Traveling to be on location with Dad had been disruptive to my own education, and my learning disability had made studying on my own very hard for me. I wanted more stability and a better education for my children, but I was embarrassed to ask for tuition for private school from my folks. They had already given me money to buy my home and helped me continue to be an artist and a stay-at-home mom, so it was extremely uncomfortable to ask them to pay for schools on top of everything else. But ultimately, I did ask, and they gave me the money for a year's tuition for both of my girls. They never gave me any guarantee from one year to the next that my kids could stay in their school. I had to ask every year, and doing so was always unnerving. I suppose I should have been more relaxed and confident that they would support the education plan year after year, but I had seen them change their minds about so many things on so many occasions, as when Dad had threatened to stop paying for my private high school when I was a teenager. More recently, both Mom and Dad had threatened to stop paying college tuition for my niece Noel, when her grades were not up to their expectations. In both cases, I advocated for them to prioritize education. In the latter case, I visited my folks in Ojai armed with books on the challenges students face in the first years of college. I convinced them that taking away funding was not a good way to encourage any student. They paid for my niece to finish college, and while Dad was alive, he paid for my daughter to go to college too.

Some of the framework I employed to set priorities for how I wanted to raise my children came from a documentary I had seen with my parents in Malibu when I was fourteen. The film was a part of Michael Apted's *Up* series. He had screened it for us. It was quite an achievement. He had interviewed fourteen kids from different socioeconomic backgrounds. The premise was built on a quote attributed to the Jesuit Saint Francis Xavier, though others say it is from Aristotle: "Give me the child until he is seven and I'll give you the man." In other words, the experiences a child has at an early age will shape the adult he or she becomes.

The fourteen subjects in the film were almost exactly my age. They were interviewed every seven years, and Apted filmed most of them from the time they were kids until they entered into their fifties. I eagerly awaited the release of each new installment. One year, one of the now grown children said something like, "I want to give my children a good education, because no matter what happens to them, no one can ever take that away from them."

The other lesson I learned from this documentary was that if you do not live in the same town as your parents, you will have a limited number of times to see them before they die, and you should be grateful for each visit. We were all very grateful to have Dad for the extra eighteen years that his new liver gave us.

Dad's transplant definitely saved his life, but a few years after having it, his drinking had become so excessive again that several people, including one of the nurses who had cared for him after the operation, asked me to say something to him. I needed to try one more time. I chose my moment carefully. I thought that if I talked with him right after he had gone on an especially big binge, his hangover might be severe enough that my words might resonate with him. It did not take long to find an occasion. I was staying with him at his estate in Ojai while my mother was on a trip to London with my daughter Kaya. Without Mom around, Dad threw a party his way; there was no fancy table setting or carefully chosen guest list. It was a really big party for the people he rode motorcycles with. This group consisted of a hundred or so of his buddies and their extended families. There were people everywhere. Many of the men had long beards; some of these guys had threaded lots of rubber bands into them, which created a kind of beard sculpture. The people drank and cavorted around in the multiple pools on the property wearing nothing but their bathing suits so that their bodies, resplendent with tattoos, made an amazing display. It was the wildest party I ever saw. Interestingly, my mom's mother, ninety-year-old Grandma Helga, who did not speak any English, was fascinated by every minute of it. She asked one of my aunts to get a man to explain what all his tattoos meant and to translate the stories into Swedish for her. Dad stayed up drinking, drugging, and partying long after I went to bed with my youngest daughter, Nora, close by my side.

The next afternoon after everyone had left, there were forgotten bathing suits and sunglasses and bottles strewn everywhere. After several hours of cleaning the place up, I sought out my dad to have a talk with him alone.

Sunset was always a good time to talk with him; and since we were alone, we had our own private gong bong, when the sun hit the horizon and was going over the edge, we took our deep breaths and, high from hyperventilating, we held hands and yelled, "Gong bong!"

As the moon came up, I told Dad how much I loved him, how much everyone loved him, and that many of us were worried about his drinking and drugging. He listened politely but was silent. I had stated my case, and there was not much more I could do. It was his life. A few days later, I called his doctor to tell her about Dad's substance abuse. When I got her on the phone, she yelled at me and angrily told me that she could not talk about his case due to privacy laws. I told her that I was not calling to get information—she did not have to say a word. I was just calling to tell her that he was drinking heavily and smoking a lot of weed. I also told her that Dad's friends in Ojai had given me her number and had asked me to call and tell her what was going on in the hope that she could do something to help him. But, as had been made clear to me on many occasions, the only person who could help Dad with his drinking was Dad himself.

After that attempt to do something about Dad's substance abuse I stopped mentioning anything about it but I knew that he was aware that I cared for him. The one time Dad really opened up to me was when he told me about a dream he had had about me. It was about two years after the operation, and we were sitting in his new penthouse in Santa Monica that had a 180-degree view of the ocean. We were alone together. Dad was drinking again but very moderately at the time. It was about half an hour before sunset, and the sky was filling with beautiful shades of pink and orange and pale gray. As we shared a bottle of wine and looked out at the ocean, he recounted what it was like coming out of the anesthesia after sixteen hours on the operating table when he had his liver transplant. He said it was like a near-death experience and that for a long time after he was in a dream state. In the dream, he felt like he was drowning in the tumultuous water of a dark and stormy ocean. He said, "You swam next to me and held my hand. You led me to an area where there was this grotto, a place that was protected by rocks that kept out the crashing waves, where the water was multicolored and calm. Once I was safe, you smiled at me and swam away. You made sure I was safe and happy."

I wanted to cry; the story of the dream truly filled me with joy. I reached out and held his hand.

Over the course of the next few years, he told me this story often, and I always felt glad that, even in his subconscious, I was able to be a comfort to him. More than two decades later, as he lay dying, I had thought of this story as I tried to comfort him again.

19

A Double Life and Alzheimer's

M Y FATHER WAS DEDICATED to my mother even though he lived a double life. He was with her most of the time, but although he spoke glowingly of her to strangers and the press, when talking to people who were truly close to him, he blamed her for any relationship in their life together that went wrong. To most everyone, Dad always appeared to be the friendly, happy, welcoming one of the two, but it was Dad who often cut people from our lives suddenly or had quasi-secret relationships with strange people whom no one in the family dared ask questions about. I was often confused when a trusted family friend was gone from our lives forever without explanation. Direct questions about the disappearance of someone with whom we had been intimate were left unanswered, and if pressed, his pat answer was, "Maj just did not like them." And that would end the conversation.

Though there was no denying that Mom was moody. Dad used her well-known bad temper as a shield to hide his own anger or sudden distrust of people they had become close to.

Mom's doctor in Santa Monica seemed reluctant to diagnose her Alzheimer's, but sometime toward the end of 2007, he said she had cognitive impairment due to some form of dementia. It wasn't a total shock; it had become obvious to everyone that she was confused. She would get lost while driving and went on shopping trips to buy the same things she had bought just the day before.

It was only when her disease caused her to become combative that Mom could no longer cope with her sense of abandonment when Dad went off with other women, and at that point, she began making her feelings about his affairs known in public. But well before her diagnosis of Alzheimer's disease explained why she no longer had normal social inhibitions, everyone knew Mom was angry, and a lot of people were afraid of her.

For years, her anger seemed irrational or was thought of as the behavior of a difficult drunk. As the disease progressed, he never knew what she was going to say or do anymore. She hit people. Dad could no longer leave her alone and go off to one of their other homes to be with some companion of his choice. He was in the sort of situation he had always sought to avoid: he was trapped.

He did not know what to do about her behavior. He could not say no to her; he never had been able to say no to her. Dad's way of dealing with her bad moods had always been to walk away and do as he pleased, but now that was not an option for him. A year after her diagnosis, he took her for a complete physical and mental evaluation to the Mayo Clinic, where it was determined that she suffered from vascular dementia and Alzheimer's. This devastating diagnosis clearly indicated that professional help would be required. But Dad resisted professional help because he didn't want strangers invading the intimate, complex life he had shared with her since he was twenty-three and she was twenty-seven.

Anyone close to her could see that Mom's bad behavior had become impossible to control. Even Dad's very loyal secretary could no longer take the strain that my mother's condition had brought to the household. One day when she felt she could not cope with Mom's flashes of anger anymore, she sent me an e-mail with details of all the many tasks that she performed in her job for the two of them and asked me if I would be willing to move to Los Angeles with my family and run Dad's office. I thought long and hard about how and when my family could move to be closer to my parents in order for me to be able to help them. There were a lot of logistics to work out. My husband was in a graduate program to become a therapist, and I felt I could not leave Seattle until my oldest daughter had graduated high school; at that point, my younger daughter would be transitioning into high school, and that would be a good time for all of us to begin this challenging new chapter in our lives.

In the interim, I flew down to Los Angeles every three weeks. Between visits, Dad was calling me often saying Mom had been yelling at him, threatening to divorce him. He confided in me partly because I was his daughter and partly because, for eight years, I had been the primary caregiver for my mother-in-law, who had recently passed away and who had also had Alzheimer's. I counseled Dad to not take Mom's angry words personally, but I firmly told him that he had to take the car keys away from her. He finally did and began to bring her everywhere with him.

It was hard to stay calm in the face of her verbal attacks, so he smoked more and more pot. He would go into his bedroom, get high, and zone out with the TV on, and while he was finding solace with his favorite drug, Mom would leave the apartment and would become lost. Dad only found out that she was missing when the police brought her home. After that had happened on a few occasions, he tried to sleep with one eye open, but after a time, his constant vigilance over her so thoroughly exhausted him that he passed out cold. While he slept, she called a taxi to drive her up to Ojai at four in the morning. He still hadn't taken her billfold from her; he always wanted to reassure her that she had plenty of money, so she always had a few hundred bucks on her.

The cab driver saw that she could pay for the expensive ride and did not ask any questions. When they arrived in Ojai, it was still dark; he let her out at the gate to the big house, and fortunately for Mom, the gardener had some extra help arriving early that day, so she was only sitting on the cold ground for about half an hour.

As she declined further, Dad was with her literally all the time. He did everything he could to keep her in a good mood. He bought her flowers several times a week and took her out to fine restaurants almost every day. But as she got worse, their lunchtime outings became unbearable for him. He was disgusted when she picked her teeth at the table and spit food out onto the floor. So he started cooking a bit. For the first time in his life, he was taking over responsibilities like grocery shopping and picking up the dry cleaning, and everywhere he went he took Mom with him. He began helping her care for herself, washing her hair, fixing her makeup, and picking out her clothes. He would make bubble baths for her surrounded by candles. He played her favorite music. They loved the score from *Pennies from Heaven*, and he would sing it to her and whistle it. They would take long drives together; it always calmed her to be going somewhere.

He had been refusing work, but he missed it a lot. He was excited when he was offered a good gig in a few episodes of a TV show in

Spain, where *Dallas* had been very popular. He planned how he could take Mom with him on location so that he could work. He wanted her to feel safe and comfortable, so Dad brought Sheila, who had worked as a maid in our family home for many years, to be Mom's caregiver.

Though Sheila knew Mom well and had real affection for her, the young woman could not handle Mom when she refused to stay in the hotel. She had no option but to bring her to watch Dad work. On the set, Mom was so disruptive that Dad had to send the two of them back home to LA.

The flight home was a disaster. They had to change planes in France, and as soon as they disembarked from the plane, Mom confidently strode off in the wrong direction. Sheila patiently struggled with her and managed to get Mom to their connecting flight. Once on board, Mom became agitated, and soon after the plane took off, she insisted that she had to talk to her husband. She walked up and down the aisles confronting passengers and asking them to give her their phones. This was making everyone uncomfortable, and the flight attendants tried to get her to sit down, which made her even more agitated. She got it into her head that there was something wrong with the flight, and she began to shout that the pilot did not know how to fly the plane. She demanded that she be allowed into the cockpit to land it herself. She told the people trying to calm her that she was a pilot and could save them. After 9/11, this kind of behavior was no longer considered eccentric; it was seen as dangerous. Somehow Sheila, with her kind, reassuring words, got Mom to stay in her seat and stop shouting. When they got home, everyone in Ojai worked together to have Mom checked into the psych ward at UCLA Medical Center.

I immediately came down to LA and went to the hospital every day to be with her until Dad came back from Europe. At that point, Dad had to face the facts, and he finally accepted that she needed professional attendants to keep an eye on her 24-7. At first he tried to keep her with him at their penthouse in Santa Monica. He hired caregivers to attend to her at home and give him a break, but as usual, he could not say no to Mom, and when she fired her attendants, he let them go and called the agency to find others. Dad kept trying new people. Greta seemed to be working well for a few weeks, but when Dad was at a doctor's appointment, I got a call from her because Mom had locked her out of the apartment. She warned me that the situation was dangerous. Hearing this from the distance of almost one thousand miles, I wished I could split myself in two and be home with my kids, who needed me, while also rushing off to be with my parents, who were having such a difficult time.

Eventually, Dad decided to move her to a facility, but he couldn't stand the idea of her being in a public place where she was locked away with a bunch of old people. The first facility she went to was in the hills between Malibu and the San Fernando Valley. It had not been updated since the early 1980s and smelled like urine. I visited her there several times and noted that she was trying to be cheerful amid her terrible confusion. It was the first time she had no access to alcohol, but by then, she was far beyond being in an alcoholic haze. Years of substance abuse had altered her permanently; she had no idea what day it was or where she was or why she was there. I knew she was physically safe, but her sadness and her longing to be with my dad broke my heart. Dad couldn't bear to visit her there.

It was plain that Dad was in a decline of a different sort. Despite his initial efforts to care for Mom and take over the basic household chores, it was not something he could maintain over time. Ultimately, without Mom to take care of him, he was a mess. His clothes were falling apart, his couch was frayed, the carpets were dirty, he was eating unhealthy food and drinking a lot.

He began working sporadically. There were guest appearances on Spanish TV; he judged beauty contests, attended autograph signings, and went on free cruises as a featured speaker. It made him happy to be active.

Another lift to his spirits was that he was being recognized for his philanthropic work for organ donation and for promoting solar energy as he did when he went to Washington, D.C., to urge Congress to extend solar investment credits. These political activities kept him busy and made him feel useful, but he missed *Dallas*, and he missed working with Patrick and Linda.

In the summer of 2010, I was finally able to move to LA and start the work of putting Dad's life back together. I had his carpets cleaned, I took his leather coat to be fixed, and I went over the books with the accountant so I could discuss the investments with Dad and my brother. My daughter Nora and I moved into an apartment just a few blocks from Dad's penthouse while my husband stayed to finish some course work for his doctorate in Seattle. While we were becoming familiar with living in Santa Monica, Dad kept us company by coming over to our place for dinner a few times a week. Although he took Mom out for lunch at least twice a week, he asked me to see her every day, which I did. He called me every evening, asking, "How is Maj doing today?"

He had decided to sell the big house in Ojai; he hardly ever went there anymore now that Mom could not be there with him. Dad asked me to interview several realtors. I narrowed the field of possibilities down according to the way he wanted to market the house and introduced them to Dad for his approval. He wanted to make sure we were marketing the property to an international clientele, with beautiful pictures in magazines and on the Internet; but even with the best, most dedicated team working to sell the property, it was hard to find a buyer—after the crash of 2008—for a home that was that big and situated in such a remote place. Ultimately, it did not sell until after he died.

The house was so huge that cleaning out all the furniture and personal effects was an ongoing process throughout the final years of Dad's life. I would drive up to Ojai a couple of times a week while my daughter was in school and bring back small, manageable loads of things that Dad could sort through. He was a pack rat, and every object or piece of clothing seemed to have an emotional tie to his life with my mother or to an important moment in his career, so it was hard for him to let anything go.

Dad loved to make an event out of everything that went on in his life, and at some point in the process of going through all their belongings, he came up with the idea of what to do with their lifetime of collecting. He was going to have a grand celebrity auction, maybe even tour around the world with their stuff to the cities where *Dallas* had been popular, making these personal items available to his fans everywhere and staying at the best hotels while on the road, with a show made up of all the quirky and interesting things he had owned, and each object had a story that he was eager to share.

A few years earlier, he had worked with an auctioneer named Darren Julien to sell one of his motorcycles. On another occasion Darren and his partner, Martin Nolan, an Irishman who was well connected in his native country, had arranged for Dad to make an appearance on an Irish talk show. They had become great friends, and Dad wanted to work and travel with them again.

Dad introduced me to Darren and Martin, and we hit it off right away. They were delightful to work with. The three of us arranged a huge auction of many of Dad's collections: hats, antiques, paintings, Western wear of every sort. While we were putting the auction together, Dad shot a test episode of the new *Dallas* and was waiting anxiously to hear if it was going to be picked up.

The auction attracted a huge amount of attention, and at the eleventh hour, Dad came up with a brilliant idea that only he would have thought of. He decided to arrive at the auction by riding a horse down one of the major streets in Beverly Hills, Wilshire Boulevard, and to have Linda Gray riding on a horse beside him. It made for quite a spectacle. No one had ridden a horse through the center of Beverly Hills since the days of Tom Mix, the costume-loving king of the cowboy western movies from the 1920s and '30s.

The pictures of Dad and Linda on horseback in Beverly Hills and the auction itself were featured in the *Los Angeles Times, The New York Times,* and *The Times* of London all in the same week. With all the publicity and activity, it felt almost like the old days. The auction was a resounding success, and despite the ever-present sorrow he felt about my mother's condition, Dad was back on his game again.

But then, just as he was feeling so much better, he got news that shook him hard. His doctor told him he had throat cancer. At first, he kept the information of his illness a secret that only a few of us knew as he tried to assess the fact of it and put it into the context of everything that was going on. He had just been on the cover of all those entertainment sections riding a stallion down Wilshire Boulevard. He had made sure that Mom had the best, most expensive care possible. After several rough years of being unable to work as he took care of Mom, he was free at last. Now this!

His life was definitely being subjected to a roller coaster of bad and good news because, days after his diagnosis, came the word he had been waiting and hoping for: *Dallas* had been picked up, and he would be reuniting with Linda and Patrick, his favorite actors and working buddies.

I went to his penthouse to talk with him about his cancer diagnosis and about what he wanted to do. I told him I would help in any way I could. When I said I would drive him to the cancer hospital in downtown LA if he wanted me to, I saw a look of desperation cross his face for just one moment. I imagined my words had caused him to envision a future during which he would be stuck in LA with me driving him to treatments and, in between treatments, visiting Mom a few times a week and watching her deteriorate. It would also mean giving up his chance to be on *Dallas* again.

That week he found the best cancer doctors in Texas, and he reminded me that he had beaten the odds before. He was starting his life over again, and nothing was going to stop him. Not even cancer. His determination filled me with awe.

There was no way of hiding his diagnosis, so he shared the information with the producers of *Dallas*. After carefully considering whether or not to let the news out to the public, Dad encouraged them to share it. For years, he had told the success story of his liver transplant, and he knew that, in so doing, he'd made a positive impact on the lives of many people who had life-threatening illnesses. The fact that he was continuing to work while getting treatment could be, he believed, an inspiration for many people facing the same frightening diagnosis.

He had not always been so forthright about his health in public. When I was writing this book, I came across a telling interview that Dad had given to a journalist from the *Edinburgh Evening News*. It started, as had so many of his other interviews, with Dad confessing to all sorts of bad behavior like taking drugs and playing practical jokes on the set. But then he went on to tell the two lies he customarily included in every interview after his liver transplant: that he had stopped drinking entirely, it was easy and that he had never cheated on his wife. The first lie was important for his legacy because so many people wanted to be just like him and would try to emulate many aspects of his fun-loving behavior; he wanted to perpetuate the myth that he had successfully, and without any difficulty at all, just quit drinking, when in fact the truth was that the addiction controlled every aspect of his daily life. The second lie was that he never cheated on my mom; that it was untrue had long been an open secret among his many friends, but he made sure that anything put in writing or in the media stated that he was a non-wandering husband. The fact is, though he wandered, he was also devoted; the very notion of divorce was appalling to him.

I can't help but wonder if he had a deal with Mom that allowed him to do anything he wanted with other women as long as he told the entire world that he was faithful. I think he would have been devastated if he had found my mother in bed with another man, but I truly believe she never slept with anyone but Dad.

———

Though Dad spent most of his last year in Texas, he kept his penthouse apartment as a pied-à-terre in Santa Monica and rented a Spanish-style house for Mom less than a mile away, where she would be watched over day and night.

He wanted the best care money could buy for his dear Majsy. He had the house filled with her furniture and the paintings she had made as a girl in Sweden. That meant she would be surrounded by many of her favorite possessions, but some of her things were too big for this smaller house, so I went with him to buy several new things too. Bringing with us the measurements for her new sitting room, Dad picked out a perfect Persian carpet for it. We also had two matching love seats in storage that had belonged to Ganny and were covered in a yellow-patterned chintz. Yellow was Mom's favorite color, so we went out to find a yellow carpet with other warm colors to go with them. Dad wanted everything there to be beautiful. And everything was.

He would come back to visit with me in LA and check on Mom every few months, but he was moving on with his own life. I got the sense that he knew his days were numbered, and he was going to have a ball with whatever time he had left.

I keep my iPhone on all night in case Mom's caregivers need to reach me and so my daughters can call me no matter what time it is, day or night. I'm always on alert for these calls, and so I was immediately wakened at 4:00 A.M. one morning when a text came in. Given the hour, I was surprised to see that it was from Dad, who was in LA on a break from shooting in Dallas. He was in good spirits. The first season of the show had gone well, and the treatment he'd gotten while it was being shot had left him cancer-free.

The text began, "Ms. Fox, you are the most BEAUTIFUL woman in the world . . ."

Dad had never as much as mentioned anything to me about the women he had been with. This was the first time he had slipped up, and I knew right away that he had texted me by mistake. He had been so distant since receiving his frightening diagnosis and starting work on the new *Dallas*. I felt that this accident provided me with an opening for some kind of communication with him. I texted him immediately: "Dad, I don't think you meant this message for me but I am OK with whoever Ms. Fox is. Maybe we should talk." He agreed.

That night, I brought dinner over to his penthouse and told him I understood his need for intimacy. He was so relieved to have everything out in the open. He had been keeping this woman a secret from me for over a year. Now he was excited to tell me all about it. They had met while the new *Dallas* was being shot and he was having treatment. He said he was in love. Once he turned that corner that allowed him to go on with his life after making sure Mom was cared for, he let himself feel love, and I wanted him to find joy.

He couldn't wait to introduce me to her, and that night, he made plans for us all to go to New York together in three weeks' time on her private jet.

Ms. Fox turned out to be quasi–age appropriate for Dad, meaning she was a year older than I am. The trip to New York was tense. I felt like I was auditioning; this woman seemed to have a great deal of influence on Dad and how he felt about everything. I wanted to be a part of his life, so her opinion of me mattered. Ms. Fox and I shared some of the same views on politics, so that eased things a bit. Still, the only thing that mattered wasn't what I felt or what she felt. What mattered was that Dad was happy.

Now that his love life was out in the open, he felt more comfortable with me, and this became particularly important when he had another spate of good and bad news: *Dallas* was picked up for another season, but then he was diagnosed with a form of leukemia. At that point, he allowed me to take him to the hospital several times a week for blood transfusions. These took many hours and gave us time to be together and to talk. He spoke a lot about his life, but nothing he said gave me the slightest sense that something was on his mind that would soon result in his begging to be forgiven.

20

Forgiveness

S OON AFTER MY FATHER'S very public memorials, I found
myself alone in his apartment. Even after the auction, his place
was amazingly full of stuff, but without Dad, it was also painfully
empty. It was my job to clean out the rest of the things my parents had
collected in the course of their very full lives, things that had now
been distilled down to the most personal objects and photographs. I
worked diligently for hours and was productive and cool and business-
like until I could no longer suppress the sadness I felt. I needed to stop
and take it all in. I sat down on my father's bed and saw, on the table
beside it, the photograph he always kept there of me with my daughter
Kaya in my lap. I had just turned forty; I wore no makeup and was
dressed plainly. I had just cut off my hair, so it was very short. All
semblance of youthful vanity was gone. I was simply a mom supporting my six-year-old child in my arms and looking lovingly at the photographer who, as I well remembered, had been Dad. He'd often told
me how much he loved that picture.

I thought about myself as a mother and what that had meant to my dad. He had always been very supportive of me when I was an actress, but he much preferred it when I became an artist and a mom. Because he had suffered the consequences of having a mother whose work as a performing artist had made it impossible for her to be a mother to him, he had made it financially possible for me to be a stay-at-home mom with a studio right in my home where I could continue to paint while remaining close to my children. He always praised the way I interacted with my kids and included them in my life as an artist.

I was still in his apartment as the light faded from the room. I did not want to leave. As long as I remained there, I could soak in his presence in the midst of all his things that were just the way he had left them. Looking back at the picture again, I thought about Dad's relationship with Ganny. There had been several big fights between my dad and his mother over the years. Most of these fights had been caused by the terrible relationship Dad had with Richard, who had also managed to alienate literally scores of people. One of them was the incredibly gifted and witty Noël Coward, who wrote a musical for Mary called *Pacific 1860*. During preparations for the show, Coward had to deal with Richard constantly. He wrote of the experience, saying of Richard, "He is a pathological case and is twisted with strange jealousies. I wish the silly ass were at the bottom of the sea."

I am sure my father would have agreed with this assessment. Richard's jealousy was especially activated by the only other man in Mary's life: her son. Richard made a point of finding fault with everything my dad did, and Dad responded by goading him. They battled endlessly. On the surface, it often seemed that Ganny sided with Richard, and yet she constantly reached out to our family and tried to find ways to include us in her life. The animosity between the two men went on for years, but there were two fights in particular that caused both my grandmother and my father so much pain that their relationship was almost completely severed.

These fights both took place in Brazil, fourteen years apart. The first happened in 1956 when my parents were still newlyweds. Dad wanted to introduce Mom to Mary and Richard after having delighted his father in Texas with his "foreign bride" as Ben called her. They flew down to Brazil, where Mary and Richard had just bought a large ranch where they planned on relaxing between Broadway shows. It had no electricity and no telephone; at night, every room was lit with kerosene lanterns. The sounds of the jungle provided a constant, soothing hum. The battery-powered turntable played glorious classical music, and the night sky was filled with unbelievably brilliant displays of stars. It was as far away from the pressures of showbiz as anyone could get.

At first, everything went very well, and Mary and Richard were overjoyed with Dad's choice of wife.

In their turn, Mom and Dad fell in love with the lush landscape of the ranch as intensely as Mary and Richard had just the year before. Life seemed simple and natural there so far from big-city life. For Mom, it brought back memories of working on the family farm in Sweden during the summers. She would bale hay all day, and at night, she rode her big, white gelding, Napoleon, with such wild abandon that sparks literally flew as the horse's hooves clattered on the cobble-stones. Dad was entranced by the ranch and thought it could be where his teenage dream of being a cowboy might finally come true. He'd had that dream when he arrived in Texas as a teenager, but Papa Ben had made him work on ranches, digging ditches to put up cattle fenc-ing instead of riding freely on the range. Here in Brazil there were plenty of workers to do the grunt work and many acres of family-owned land to ride on. Seeing her son so happy, Mary suggested that they change their plans of moving to New York and stay in Brazil permanently to run the place. For a few days, my parents considered the offer. It would mean changing the entire course of the lives they had planned. Dad would not continue his acting career, and Mom would stop working as a designer so they could live a bucolic life and not have to worry about money.

But the arrangement would also mean that between shows, Mary and Richard would come to the ranch and would be the true owners. Mom and Dad would be working for them. Even in this beautiful, calm setting and despite all Mom's effort to distract them and make happy conversation, Richard's constant criticism of Dad made the idea of living together intolerable. They fought, and my father took his bride and left Brazil abruptly, vowing never to speak to Richard or Mary again. My parents kept to their initial plan of continuing their respective careers in New York. They were determined to establish their lives and careers without any help from Mary or her controlling husband.

About a year later, Mom became pregnant with me and realized how very far away she was from her family in Sweden, so she made an attempt to broker a détente between Dad and Mary and Richard, who were back in New York by this time.

After a long phone conversation with my mother, Ganny knew what an ally Mom would be in any disagreement, and thus began our uneasy but constant connection with Mary and Richard until the next visit to Brazil.

When I was thirteen years old, I began a regular correspondence with Ganny, who had semiretired and was again living in Brazil. In the letters, I asked her if she would just be a plain old grandma to me because I could not speak Swedish and therefore could not really talk to my mother's mother. Ganny was overjoyed to be connected with her family again and she responded with wonderful letters. She tried to get into the spirit of being a grandmother without being too humbled by the role, she was always signing them, "Your grandmother, Mary Martin." In these letters, she wrote about how happy and relaxed she and Richard were in Brazil, and in every letter she wrote me and my parents, she entreated us to visit. Dad was hesitant to go, and it wasn't just his own relationship with Richard that gave him pause. He still got angry when recalling the way Richard had picked on Preston a few years earlier when my brother was only three years old. At that time, Mary and Richard had wanted to show my mother a needle-point rug they had designed for their very elegant dining room. My mother was nervous that we kids would mess up the precious new rug, and sure enough, my brother spilled ice cream on it. Later, writing about the incident, Ganny portrayed it as a humorous scene in which she and Richard made light conversation to theatrically ignore what had happened until the French maid had cleaned it all away. Dad remembered the experience differently. He was convinced that Richard had tripped Preston so the boy could not help but drop his ice cream. He had never forgiven Richard for this, but he finally said he would bring us all to Brazil to stay with Mary and Richard.

I have magical memories of our first few days at the ranch, like the long horseback ride into a jungle filled with monkeys swaying from the trees above us and giant blue iridescent butterflies floating in the thick, humid air. After what seemed like hours, we came to an isolated village where a portable record player was incongruously playing a song by the Beatles, "Sun King," that had one stanza in English and one in Portuguese. As we entered the village we heard the sweet lyrics: "Here comes the sun king, everybody's laughing, everybody's happy."

But the enchantment was broken as drastically as it had been during my parents' first visit to Brazil. Richard began to pick on Preston in just the same way he had tortured Dad as a child, but it was a thousand times worse for Dad because he wanted to protect his son.

Richard was drinking tumblers of gin, pretending it was water he needed for his health. This is how Dad described the Richard he encountered: "After eleven o'clock in the morning, he was impossible. Later I found out one of the reasons Richard liked Brazil so much was that you could buy almost any medication over the counter, including amphetamines."

According to Dad, Richard was taking the drugs by the handful.

My brother, Preston, was ten years old at the time, and Richard, along with the butler, Ernest, were constantly reprimanding him and criticizing his table manners, so much so that my brother threw up his meals. One night he got up from the table because he was feeling sick again and stumbled on his way out. Just as he did this, Richard called after him, telling him he was clumsy. Dad confronted Richard, accusing him of tripping his son, just as he had years before. Dad could not stand my brother being hurt by Richard, and he was incensed that his mother remained silent. We all stared at Dad as he stood up and shoved his chair back from the table. He focused all his rage at his mother and yelled at her, saying, "You're not my mother, and you never were!"

She and Richard stood up too, and they all went off into another room where they continued to shout at one another. Mom hustled my brother and me off to the guesthouse well away from the upset.

The next morning, we left Mary and Richard's ranch and we were on a flight home soon after. My father must have felt he had failed my brother, and I am sure he felt deeply sorry that he had not stepped in to protect him sooner. After this incident, my father would never again be persuaded to interact with Richard, and we did not talk to or see his mother again until Richard died a year later.

As I was cleaning Dad's apartment after he died, I found a letter sitting on his desk. It was written in red ink on several pages of long, yellow legal paper in my grandmother's distinctive handwriting. Ganny had written it a few months after the fight occurred in Brazil. Reading it, I understood how terrible the confrontation had been for both of them. As she wrote, "We literally stripped each other's soul apart."

It was the first time I had ever seen the letter, though Dad must have looked at it often after receiving it more than forty years before. She wrote:

> *I know we think differently about life, God, love, forgiveness and probably always will. But in my heart or soul—whatever you wish to call it—I cannot live with myself without saying—"I forgive Larry."*

She then addressed the words he'd said in fury:

> *You are not my mother and you never were. The thing I must deal with is that what you spoke is the truth and the truth hurts. I must admit that decisions I made all those years ago were the wrong decisions as far as they concerned you. I didn't fight to keep you, my son. And now I come face to face with the fact that you have lived—lo these many years—with a hurt, with the sense that you were an unwanted little boy. I ask for your forgiveness. Until now I have never*

known what it means when they say, forgive us our trespasses as we
forgive those who trespass against us.

    Even if I weren't your mother and was just a friend—and so help
you darling one—I am both—I love you.

Your mom

This letter had been written forty years earlier, yet my father had always kept it and, in his final days, had placed it on his desk. I could see from the traces of fingerprints that he'd read it again and again. And I could literally see how much it meant to him because certain words had been blurred and stained by his tears.

The letter was a treasure. The fact that Dad had kept it so close at hand made it a window into the true feelings of two people who had so carefully crafted everything the world knew about them. For the first time, I understood why, in the final hours of his life, my father's mind was focused on forgiveness.

Perhaps, ever since his grandmother died, the little boy inside of him was convinced that he had done wrong. Because he'd made a practice of handling his various transgressions by making light of them, he was not a man who knew how to say, "I'm sorry." All his life, no matter what he did, no matter how adept he had been at getting everyone else to forgive him, it struck me that he had never been able to forgive himself.

I had been there in his last coherent moments when, as I realize now, all the façades had fallen away and we were alone together, he no longer felt he had to perform.

I remember watching the monitor after I told him, "You're a very good boy"—words that a mother would say to her son. I remember that his breathing had calmed and that I saw his heart rate become normal. These monitors had verified that the outward calm extended deep within him.

Those words—*you're a very good boy*—had provided absolution. They had given him the essential belief that he had been forgiven for everything. They had allowed my amazing, restless, loving dad to find the peace he had never sought but had always needed.

Acknowledgments

I want to thank Elizabeth Kaye, my coauthor, with all my heart. As a person with learning disabilities I never imagined that I could ever write a book. She patiently mentored me and helped me tell this story, and in doing so enabled me to find my writer's voice. Thank you to Thomas Dunne Books, especially Executive Editor Laurie Chittenden, who knows all about Texans, Melanie Fried, associate editor, who was very patient with all my questions about the writing process, and Rob Kirkpatrick, who believed in this project.

I send kind wishes to my fellow traveler on this adventure, my brother, Preston Hagman, and his children, Noel, Tara, and Becca. Also my aunts, my beloved BB, Lilimore, and Heller.

This story would never have happened without all of you who watched my acting family members doing their work. Dad and Ganny loved you all.

I want to thank all my friends who have been so supportive to me throughout the writing of this book. I am very fortunate, and there are too many of you to name, but I can't let people close this book without acknowledging a few of you. First, thank you to my rock, Kevin Murphy, who is always there when I need him. I want to thank my father's best friends, Roger Phillips and Henri Kleiman. Others who helped me are: the Fondas; the Brewer family; Philip Mengel; Barbara Baumann and Johan Feldbusch; Laura Hubber; Richard and Jasper Bangs; Annie Whitney; the entire Quinn family; my improv group from the Comedy Store, along with their wives. Also my neighbors in Santa Fe, Seattle, and Santa Monica, who have fed me body and soul. I also want to thank Santa Monica College, especially the dedicated English teachers, the staffs of the Learning Disabilities Program and High Tech Training Center, and Patti Davis, leader of the Beyond Alzheimer's support group at UCLA Medical Center.